GRAB YOUR SECATEURS.

BEAUTY IS EVERYWHERE.

OPEN YOUR EYES. CHOOSE HOW YOU WANT TO SEE. CHOOSE BEAUTY AND THE ABUNDANT, MYSTERIOUS WORLD WILL OPEN ITSELF TO YOU. YOU'LL FIND IT EVERYWHERE. I LEARNED THIS FROM MY GRANDMOTHER, OLGA. HER IDEA OF BEAUTY WASN'T GRAND VIEWS AND GORGEOUS ARCHITECTURE. IT WAS ROCKS SHE'D FOUND IN A PADDOCK, SWEET PEAS GROWING UP A FENCE AND POPLAR TREES IN THE DISTANCE. SHE LIVED IN A STATE OF AWE.

EVERYTHING IS CONNECTED.

WE ARE PART OF A GLOBAL WEB. THE HAWKESBURY RIVER FLOWING OUTSIDE MY WINDOW IS THE HUDSON RIVER IN NEW YORK AND THE GANGES IN INDIA. NOTHING EXISTS IN ISOLATION. REMOVE ONE TINY PIECE OF SILK FROM THE WEB OF EXISTENCE AND THE WHOLE STRUCTURE IS UNDERMINED. THINK ABOUT IT.

A GARDEN IS NOT AN OBJECT, BUT A PROCESS.

THESE ARE NOT MY WORDS. THEY'RE IAN HAMILTON FINLAY'S. THEY SAY EVERYTHING, THOUGH. A GARDEN IS A NEVER-ENDING QUEST, A LOVE AFFAIR WITH THE LAND, A DEEPLY PERSONAL EXPRESSION OF CONNECTION BETWEEN A PERSON AND THEIR ENVIRONMENT. IT'S A RELATIONSHIP THAT CHANGES EVERY SECOND, EVERY HOUR, EVERY WEEK AND EVERY YEAR. HOW GLORIOUS, TO BE INVOLVED IN SUCH A PURSUIT!

WE ARE NATURE.

THERE IS NO SEPARATION. WE HAVE QUALITIES THAT MAKE US UNIQUE, AS DO BIRDS, PIGS AND TREES. WE INFLUENCE OUR SURROUNDINGS AND CHANGE OUR ENVIRONMENT, JUST AS TERMITES IMPACT THE LANDSCAPE BY CREATING TRACKS, TUNNELS AND NESTS. VIEWING OURSELVES AS JUST ONE OF MANY SPECIES ON THE PLANET MIGHT HELP US CHANGE THE FOUNDATION OF OUR INFLUENCE FROM CONTROL TO COLLABORATION.

EVERYTHING DIES.

THE TALLEST, OLDEST TREES WILL ONE DAY DIE. I WILL DIE. THE ANT WILL DIE. ACKNOWLEDGING DEATH IS A GOOD WAY TO LIVE. LOVE WHILE YOU CAN. CARE WHILE YOU CAN. GROW WHILE YOU CAN.

PLAY.
EXPERIMENT.
OBSERVE.
LEARN.

THERE ARE NO RULES WHEN IT COMES TO GARDENING. YOU CAN READ ALL YOU WANT ABOUT HOW TO DO EVERYTHING RIGHT, BUT THE ONLY WAY TO LEARN IS BY DOING; ANY EXPERIENCED GARDENER WILL TELL YOU THIS. HERE'S A FACT: YOUR NEW PLANT WILL DIE ONE DAY. IT MIGHT BE TOMORROW, NEXT WEEK, OR NOT FOR A FEW YEARS, BUT IT WILL HAPPEN. DON'T BE SCARED. EMBRACE IT, CARE FOR IT AND LOVE IT. WHEN IT DIES, TRY TO UNDERSTAND WHY, AND TRY AGAIN. AND AGAIN.

LISTEN TO THE TREES.

TREES ARE WISE; THEY KNOW MANY THINGS WE DON'T. I REVERE THEM. I PRESS MY EAR TO
THEIR TRUNKS, LISTEN TO THEIR STORIES AND WHISPER MY THANKS AND ENCOURAGEMENT.
I AM A WORSHIPPER OF TREES. I RECOMMEND IT.

QUESTION EVERYTHING. KNOW NOTHING.

EVERYTHING IS QUESTIONABLE, ABSOLUTELY EVERYTHING. WHAT IS THIS LIVING BUSINESS ALL ABOUT? WHY DO I WANT TO BUILD A WALL OR GROW A PARTICULAR PLANT? HOW CAN I BE MORE IN TUNE WITH THE WORLD AROUND ME? ARE BULL ANTS REALLY AGGRESSIVE OR DO THEY JUST LOOK ANGRY? QUESTIONS ARE MORE IMPORTANT THAN ANSWERS, AND KNOWING IS OVERRATED. WHEN IN DOUBT, ASK. BE CURIOUS.

ALL PLANTS ARE EQUAL.

PLANTS ARE LIVING, BREATHING, EXQUISITE BEINGS. THEY ARE ABOVE TRENDS AND FASHION. ALL PLANTS ARE EQUAL. ALL PLANTS ARE BEAUTIFUL. ALL PLANTS ARE WORTHY OF LOVE AND ATTENTION. PLANTS ARE NOT OBJECTS.

IF PLANTS DON'T EXIST, WE DON'T EXIST.

DON'T FORGET THIS. EVER. CULTIVATE A WINDOW GARDEN, A TINY COURTYARD OR A FEW POTS ON YOUR DESK AT WORK AND REMEMBER THAT THESE LIVES EXIST IN DEEP CONNECTION TO YOUR OWN. PLANTS, AND LOVE, MAKE THE WORLD GO AROUND.

LOVE YOUR MOTHERS.

YOUR HUMAN MOTHER AND YOUR MOTHER EARTH ARE ONE AND THE SAME. TO LOVE IS TO CARE, PROTECT AND RESPECT. EXPRESS YOUR LOVE EVERY DAY THROUGH YOUR WORDS, THOUGHTS AND ACTIONS. YOUR MOTHERS, FATHERS, SISTERS AND BROTHERS WILL THANK YOU. TODAY AND TOMORROW.

TO WENDY AND PETER, FOR SHOWING ME HOW TO GROW. GR
TO THE REMARKABLE WOMEN WHO HAVE SHAPED ME. DS

THE PLANTHUNTER
TRUTH, BEAUTY, CHAOS, AND PLANTS

GEORGINA REID WITH PHOTOGRAPHY BY DANIEL SHIPP

TIMBER PRESS
PORTLAND, OREGON

HOME TRUTHS

LIFE WITH PLANTS

INTRODUCTION

I didn't know until a few years ago that my name, Georgina, means 'farmer' or 'tiller of the earth'. Neither did my parents when they named me all those years back, but they were spot on. I've always instinctively been drawn to the dirt. I like sitting in it, I was constantly covered in it when I was a child, and I love all the lives that exist because of it.

When my parents told me they were selling our family farm, I wandered around the paddocks crying. I lay face down on the earth, arms spread wide. I wanted to melt into the land that was the foundation of my life, to physically embody the deep emotional connection I felt to it. I realised then what I'd only suspected previously – my attachment to the earth and all that grows from it is a deeply important aspect of my life and my truth.

I was twenty-six then and working as a landscape designer. Although I had spent all of my early years gardening or working on the family farm, a career in horticulture and landscape design wasn't ever my plan. I remember doing one of those career quizzes when I was a teenager. It told me I should become a florist. With hindsight I can see it wasn't far off the mark, but at the time, with my only experience of floristry consisting of hot pink gerberas in rural shopping centres, I was horrified. I wanted a 'proper' career. I continued on my short-lived 'important-sounding' career trajectory.

Not long after I finished university, the puzzle pieces fell into place. Plants, unlike my just-completed communications degree, were where my heart lay. I decided, driven predominantly by intuition, to study horticulture and landscape design. I've never once looked back, and my ideas about what constitutes an important career have since withered like a cyclamen leaf in the blazing sun.

Until recently, I hadn't ever had a garden of my own. I have designed many, worked regularly in my parent's garden, and pottered around in a rented courtyard, yet I was primarily a gardener of the mind. My curiosity (and perhaps the lack of a physical space to unearth answers in) led me towards questions of place, plants and connection. I began asking people what drew them to plants and why they gardened. Very few could answer coherently. It just was something they did, they told me. I couldn't answer my own questions either, so I continued digging. I had a sense that connecting with plants – whether gardening, bushwalking, painting or writing – is both deeply intuitive and an incredibly important source of nourishment for the human spirit. I wondered if the lessons we learn from plants and nature can transform our relationships with ourselves, each other and the world around us.

Eventually I managed to give the piles of questions and musings scribbled on scraps of paper some coherent form. I created an online publication called *The Planthunter*. For me, this was an act of gardening. I was creating a place where questions about the relationship between nature and culture could be asked, composted and chewed over. Since then, I've learned a lot, and my world has expanded in ways I could never have imagined, but the initial questions that were the seeds of *The Planthunter* remain as relevant to me now as they were then. Even more so.

I am deeply worried about the current state of life on our planet. I don't understand a lot of things and I certainly don't claim to have any grand solutions. I care, though.

Passionately. My way of expressing my love for the earth and my hope for the future is to garden. The values that are important to me, the way of being in the world that feels right, and glimpses of the beauty and mystery of what it means to be alive, are nurtured when I connect with the earth beneath my feet. Gardening is an accessible, hopeful, and incredibly powerful act.

I'm writing this from a ramshackle boatshed on the banks of the Hawkesbury River. Outside my door lies a patch of dirt – my first-ever garden. I'm reminded each time I wander through it that I can do something good for the earth. I can grow hope and I can nurture beauty. It's a place that reminds me that my role is one of collaborator, not dictator. It's a place where I can cultivate my relationship to the world around me.

The connections and perspectives grown in gardens are not contained by boundaries and fences. They're shared – passed down from parent to child, or between friends and neighbours, through plant cuttings, excess garden produce or flowers. They're seeded into the ways we see the world around us. They burrow inwards too. Towards truth. 'Gardening ... embodies more saliently than any other practice the truth of the relation between human beings, their world, and the "ground" from which the "gift" of this world comes,' writes David E Cooper in *A Philosophy of Gardens*.

Despite this, gardening is often reduced to the practical and horticultural. It becomes a set of tasks: mow, prune, kill, repeat. The deeper importance and value of the act rarely warrants a mention in the places that gardening itself is mentioned (a limited landscape to begin with). At the same time, for many complex social, cultural and economic reasons, there is less and less opportunity for the many Australians who live in cities to get their hands dirty.

The fuzzy-edged filter of nostalgia makes it easy to lament the past as some kind of golden era, or suggest that if everyone had a garden the world would be a happier, kinder place. Maybe it would. But this world, right now, is all there is. Perhaps it's time to reimagine what it means to garden, and recognise the gifts of hope, beauty and truth the act offers.

Gardening is simply the act of conversing with the natural world through plants. It's a framework for seeing and engaging with the world, based on a deep appreciation of and respect for natural processes – a desire to create beauty, a drive to care, and an eye to the future. Gardening is not limited to backyards. It can happen anywhere and everywhere: from balconies to bathrooms, street verges to paddocks, rooftops and walls. A painting, a pot plant, a landscape, a play or an essay – all these can be gardened. When seen in this way, opportunities to engage with and care for the natural world abound. They're everywhere. Hope, beauty and truth are everywhere.

If you hadn't already guessed, I'm a meanderer. Straight lines and clear definitions are not my thing. This book is many things. It's a collection of stories about people who have affected, shaped, inspired and challenged me in my journey towards understanding what it is to be a tiny piece of silk in the grand spider web of existence. It's an ode to the act of gardening (although you'll learn nothing about pruning, pests and diseases or growing vegetables). It's a celebration of the exceptional and ordinary ways people engage with the world around them through plants. It's a bunch of questions and not many answers. Finally, and simply, it's a song of deep love and reverence for this world, our Mother Earth.

This song began quietly whispering its tune thirty-eight years ago in a garden surrounded by low, rolling hills of Australian farmland. It continues now, a little stronger, in the wallaby-ravaged beginnings of a garden by the river, in the bushland I traipse through behind our house, on the streets of the city, in my dreams for the future and my memories of the landscape of my childhood.

This song – my song – calls me home.

The gangsta gardener

RON FINLEY

RON FINLEY IS A GARDENER, ACTIVIST AND ARTIST WHO GAINED
INTERNATIONAL ATTENTION AFTER GIVING A TED TALK ABOUT HIS
STREET GARDEN. HE'S A FASCINATING, NO-BULLSHIT CHARACTER,
WHOSE ACTIONS HAVE INSPIRED COUNTLESS HOME AND
COMMUNITY GARDEN PROJECTS THE WORLD OVER, HIGHLIGHTING
THE POWER OF GARDENING AS AN AGENT OF CHANGE.

COLOUR REFERENCE: FIRESTICKS (*Euphorbia tirucalli* 'Firesticks')   LOCATION: SOUTH CENTRAL LOS ANGELES, USA

In 2010, Ron Finley decided to pull up the turf on the nature strip outside his house in South Central Los Angeles and replace it with an edible garden. The local authorities fined him, even issuing an arrest warrant. Ron fought back and demanded the right to garden and grow food in his neighbourhood. The city authorities backed off and Ron's story of creating opportunity and beauty through gardening made its way around the globe. 'I didn't choose gardening. The garden chose me.'

Beauty, not just food, was the driving force behind Ron's street garden. 'I wanted people to be assaulted by beauty. I wanted to walk outside my house and be kissed by butterflies and hummingbirds. If you see ugly all the time, you think it's normal. But imagine seeing beauty everywhere you go. Beauty happens by design, just like ugly does.'

Ron's garden is the embodiment of his ideas about the cultivation and importance of beauty. His backyard consists of a pool that is filled with plants and art instead of water. Plants grow in pots, out of buckets, on makeshift shelves, in shopping trolleys and up walls. 'There is no trash, there's just art waiting to happen, that's how I look at stuff.'

His famous street garden is also abundant. There are fruit trees, vegetables, herbs and flowers. He has been building the soil up for years. 'Did you notice how high my soil is?' It is so high that he has had to install timber edging to stop it washing away. 'To me, soil is magical.' Frames made of woven sticks hold compost piles, support climbing plants and provide shelter for a small seating area. It's humming with life.

'Last week some neighborhood kids came by with their friends, sat in the little hut and ate nasturtiums. When I saw their mum I said, "What have you created?" And she said, "Me? That's you. You've done this. You changed my kids – they're running around eating flowers out of the garden." How can you not be happy with that? It just shows if you put good in, that's what you get out.'

This is a 'take what you want/need' garden. But there are rules. 'I don't like people taking my flowers. See on the corner up there? All of that is planted with sunflowers and artichokes. It's like an art piece for me. When people pass by on the street, I want them to see this beauty. The fourteen-foot sunflowers are magnificent, but people desecrate them. They cut the sunflowers for themselves or just break them. It's almost like beauty makes them feel uncomfortable.'

Ron was a loner as a child. 'I stayed in the house a lot until they thought there was something wrong with me and told me to go outside. I went outside and I never came back in.' Yard work was his 'side hustle' as a teenager. 'I'd mow lawns, clean out people's gardens, stuff like that.' His perspective has always been his own, unhindered by conformity. 'Being dyslexic, you just see shit differently to start with. I learn by touching and doing, not reading what's written on a board. My whole thing is, if it's ugly and it don't work, fix it.'

While Ron is known primarily as someone involved with food and edible gardening, his garden means much more than that to him. 'This garden is not about food. It's about people, it's all about realising that you can design the life you want to live and not live the one that's been designed for you.'

He points to the practice of growing grass on street verges as an example. 'No-one questions it. No-one asks why we're not growing food instead of grass. We're like ants and this is our maze. The maze is designed for one thing only – commerce. It's not designed for people. We have choices. We've been conditioned to accept the situation we're in, therefore we can be conditioned to do something else. We can be conditioned to not use plastic, we can be conditioned to give a fuck about our neighbours, about the earth.'

'What do we value? Where do our values come from? Why do we pledge allegiance to a flag and not to Mother Nature? We've been taught to value what people want us to value, not what's really important.'

He talks about water, soil and air: three invaluable things that sustain all life on earth, yet are in many ways invisible. 'Why haven't we been trained to value water? Because you turn on your faucet and out it comes. This kind of thinking has got us fucked up. People don't think they need to think about where their water comes from, where their food comes from.'

Ron makes change and reconnection sound simple. 'It *is* simple. There's grass out there, I'm going to take it out and grow food. Easy. People have fed themselves for millennia. It's natural. How difficult can it truly be? Why is this garden so special? It shouldn't be.'

The one thing Ron's garden doesn't have but needs, he tells me, is pole dancers. 'I'm working on that,' he laughs. 'We have to make gardening sexy. Once you convert something desolate to something beautiful and awe-inspiring, it gets you. The soil seduces you. It's simple.'

Ron is an accidental activist. He just grew a garden on the street outside his house, fuelled by a desire to create beauty and change in his immediate neighbourhood. He just wanted to 'grow some shit'. He had no idea who his actions and ideas would reach or how far they would spread. He talks tough, but he's soft enough for tears. 'I get tears. Big tears sometimes. I'm tired, but elated.'

IDEAS OF BEAUTY

RON FINLEY ON HOPE
AND OPPORTUNITY

Fuck hope. What can you do with hope? Can you go to the bank with pockets filled with hope and cash it in? You can't use hope for nothing. People need opportunity, people don't need no hope. You've got a cupload of opportunity and a boatload of hope, what one will you take? The cup of opportunity. I guess you can say I have hope, but I'm not a hope seller, I'm an opportunity seller.

I have the opportunity to do this and I have the opportunity to change people's lives. I didn't know this was going to happen. I'm elated, and I'm honoured. It's weighty as hell sometimes, but the fact that I know that there's people out there whose lives have been changed makes me very happy. People have listened to me and heard what they needed to hear to change their lives. And it's in real time. It's not like I planted a seed and had to wait twenty years for the tree to fruit. It's happening right now.

A post-industrial wal

BILL HENSON

QUESTIONS OF BEAUTY, MYSTERY, ORDER AND CHAOS ABOUND IN
AUSTRALIAN ARTIST BILL HENSON'S GARDEN. AS WELL AS BEING
AN INTERNATIONALLY RENOWNED PHOTOGRAPHER, BILL IS ALSO
A PASSIONATE GARDENER. HIS HOME AND PHOTOGRAPHY STUDIO
ARE EMBRACED BY A LUSH AND LAYERED WILDERNESS. IT'S HARD
TO KNOW WHERE THE GARDEN BEGINS AND ENDS, AND THAT'S THE
WAY BILL LIKES IT.

COLOUR REFERENCE: BEGONIA (*Begonia* spp.)   LOCATION: NORTHCOTE, AUSTRALIA

ed garden

IDEAS OF BEAUTY

Bill Henson was a surprise. I had been told he had a good garden, but I had no idea of the depth of his obsession. I presumed art had a controlling hand over Bill's heart, but I was wrong. He's a very serious garden maker, garden lover and garden thinker. 'Gardens, books and art are the three fixed points with which I move the world. They're the trifecta.'

Bill's garden is an entire universe. It's an incredibly atmospheric space, imbued with a sense of mystery and beauty only he could create. Walls are invisible, movement in neighbouring buildings can be heard but not seen, and the sky is framed by a tumble of tree canopies. Pepper trees (*Schinus molle*), Canary Island date palms (*Phoenix canariensis*), figs, cypress trees and cordylines wriggle and shove, elbowing their way towards the light. Layers of underplanting fill the space, dripping down walls and climbing up tree trunks.

This garden is a wild and beautiful expression of Bill's creative process — making, meandering and questioning. 'Gardening is finding a form outside your body through which to articulate things which ultimately you don't fully understand.'

'You find out what things are about through trying to make them, create them. That's how I am with my photographs. I'm never quite sure what it's going to look like. You apply yourself intellectually, but it's the process of trying to make the picture, or the garden, that leads you to understanding what it's about.'

Bill is not just a gardener of the mind — he is as physical as he is cerebral. In 2006, he bought the mechanic's workshop and car park next to his warehouse home. He excavated the car park and ordered sixty tonnes of Coldstream stone, which he used to build the tall, dry-stone retaining walls that are now almost completely hidden by foliage. 'It took me a couple of weeks,' he says, very casually. 'Fitting rocks together is exciting. I could do it all day.'

The walls frame a sea of gravel that runs the length of the space. It's the void to the garden's mass, the order to nature's exuberance. Bill rakes the gravel every morning. 'In a way, the gravel is the known world. And then you climb up into the rocks and you find the wildness. For me, that tug between human control and nature constantly reclaiming the landscape is what I like. I've never found pure wilderness very interesting. Walking through Tasmania or the South Island of New Zealand is very beautiful but not actually interesting to me. But coming across a pair of old stone gates in an overgrown landscape on the outskirts of Rome, that's kinda sexy.'

I find wilderness endlessly interesting, but I get his point. There's something about the tension between order and chaos – the contrast of form and wildness in a landscape – that creates an attraction like no other. The beauty of Bill's wild planting is made more pronounced, more dramatic and more mysterious by being constrained by walls, boundaries and gravel. 'My ideal garden tends towards wilderness. You have the known world, which in my case is the gravel, and then it heads off into the hinterland, where you're not sure where it begins or ends. Magic, mystery, darkness. That's what animates the speculative capacity in people. It forces them to think.'

For Bill, gardening is a drug. It's a form of meditation and 'one of the most ancient and greatest pathways into contemplation'. Sometimes he'll head down in the morning to rake the gravel or water his endless collection of pots and he won't return for four hours. Constructive manual labour is important to him. He waters all his plants by hand every day (many of which are trees in huge terracotta pots), offhandedly mentioning how he can wrangle nearly any sized pot and plant with a crowbar 'like the Egyptians', and tells me about installing bird's nest ferns (*Asplenium australasicum*) in the tops of the trees. 'It's a bit precarious.'

Many of the plants in Bill's garden have been rescued. 'I can't stand the disappearance of the city's gardens. Every time they pull down an old house they bulldoze the garden. It's destroying the city. There are so many things that could be saved.' So Bill saves them. He has rescued accidentally bonsaied radiata pines (*Pinus radiata*) that were growing in tin cans in a run-down nursery, an old cypress from a building site, and more. He tells me about a recent mission to a nursery he'd visited as a child. 'When they bulldozed it, I went out with my friend who has a digger and a truck and saved a whole bunch of ferns. They would be hundreds of years old.'

There's always room for more plants in Bill's unruly garden. 'A big, overgrown garden in the middle of the city is the ultimate luxury.' He likes the country, but there's something about the containment and humanity of the city that appeals to him. It's like he needs structure to push against.

For Bill, gardening and making art are one and the same. He has committed himself fully – mind and body – to both. Both are acts of construction. Both are about creating mood and stimulating emotion. Both are about using beauty as a tool for discovery and speculation.

'The best experience you can have with art is to go away with more questions than you came with, even though everything today is about certainty and exactitude and measuring. To encounter the great untidiness in good art is like going into a garden where you can't see the beginning or the end of the space.'

Bill Henson's garden, then, is the work of a great artist.

A POST-INDUSTRIAL WALLED GARDEN

BILL HENSON ON ART, EVOLUTION AND BEAUTY

On photography and gardening

Making pictures and gardening both depend entirely on nature. If I'm working with a model, I can't control what they'll do and how their appearance changes, and how it makes their relationship with me and the camera, and the dynamic, more or less compelling. You can't quantify it and you can't control it. It is the same in the garden.

On evolution

The definition of a garden is that it's man-made. But beyond a certain point, a garden is its own thing. It's constantly evolving at a cellular level. The light, the weather – every day it's different. It's just like working with a model, even in the so-called controlled environment of the studio. Even asking a model to turn their head to the left or the right – there's a million ways that can happen, and a million things that can suggest. They overlap on many, many levels. Things are being revealed to you all the time.

On beauty

There's a great quote by writer and poet Peter Schjeldahl. I might be paraphrasing, but it goes something like this: 'Beauty presents a stone wall to the thinking mind. It makes a case for the sacred and then wins that case, suddenly and irrationally.'

Healing gardens

TOPHER DELANEY

TOPHER DELANEY IS A CONCEPTUAL ARTIST WITH AN OUTPUT THAT
SPANS GARDENS, INTERIOR AND EXTERIOR ART INSTALLATIONS,
PHOTOGRAPHY AND PAINTING. HER WAY IS ONE OF GENEROSITY,
CURIOSITY AND SPIRIT, AND HER WORK IS FOCUSED ON ONE THING
ONLY – TRANSFORMATION. 'NOTHING MORE, NOTHING LESS.'
IT SOUNDS SIMPLE BUT THERE IS NOTHING SIMPLE OR EASY
TO DEFINE ABOUT TOPHER DELANEY.

COLOUR REFERENCE: CHINESE LANTERN (*Abutilon* x *hybridum*)   LOCATION: DOGPATCH, USA

Topher Delaney makes gardens. Not as a landscape architect, although she trained as one, but as an artist. I read her book *10 Landscapes* during my first job in a landscape architecture firm and was intrigued by her dramatic and curious work. Her unconstrained exploration of what a garden is and can be in relation to a personal and environmental narrative was unlike anything I'd seen before. Her output spans private and public gardens, as well as healing gardens at hospitals. Transformation is the common thread running through each space.

Topher was born in the US but spent her early years in France. She studied cultural anthropology in New York before relocating to San Francisco to explore ideas of landscape and place. 'I wanted to work on how people make a sanctuary of their land. How they take their narratives from where they came from and embed them in the landscape. To me, California was the place to do this.' She studied landscape architecture at Berkeley. 'I didn't really enjoy it, but I needed the degree. I didn't understand what they were all doing, it was very mysterious.'

After she graduated, she became a gardener. 'I realised I really loved plants but didn't know anything about them. I was completely ignorant. I didn't know how to build anything, do anything.' Topher set about learning – her way, of course. She gardened, and then started a construction company. 'I had about forty people working for me, building streets, sidewalks, that kind of thing'. She used the income to support her art commissions, many of which involved gardens. 'I love the process of gardens. Taking care of plants and gardens is taking care of people – it's all the one continuum.'

Topher's studio, Delaney + Chin, is in the semi-industrial Dogpatch district of San Francisco. Outside, a series of seats and concrete planters filled with a tangle of roses, geraniums and other greenery line the wall. Inside is an Aladdin's cave of artworks, materials and stories. Woollen rugs with barcode designs line the floor. Each rug has a message – usually related to transformation – contained within the barcode. A metal screen, with an aerial plan of the French garden Vaux-le-Vicomte perforated into it, leans against a wall. Artworks in various stages of completion fill the space.

Topher and I load two trays of rosemary cuttings in cups into the boot of her car and head to the University of San Francisco's medicinal botanical garden. Delaney + Chin designed and installed the project in 2009 and still maintain it. 'It's not enormous, it's public and it's all about diversity of medicinal plants.' The garden is a botanical necklace of sorts –

a series of beautiful and medicinal jewels wrapping around the exterior of the building. Angled, rusted steel walls with the plants' botanical names inscribed on them contain the abundance and define the space.

'It's really important what you do in these spaces. It's got to have intention, it's got to have diversity. The challenge is to take uneventful spaces, like this one was, and transform them into places that speak to people, everyday people. I can show you really fancy things I've done, but that's not the point. The point is to look at what an average person's experience is. Not the wealthy. Everyone.' As if on cue, a couple walking their dog through the space stop to look at and touch the plants.

Topher points to a new development across the road. Small trees are under-planted with masses of grasses and shrubs. It's a standard, nondescript landscape, typical of many newly designed public spaces. 'That's what you get with landscape architecture. There's no recognition of site or sacredness of land. What part of the land do we know about from that planting, that design? All those people who live over there come over here. Because this is a real garden. They wander around and discuss it like they never discuss that place. What I don't understand is who wins out of creating spaces like that? Who prospers?'

We take the trays of rosemary into the building. They are cuttings from the garden, saved by Topher for the university's staff members. She chats to the slightly bemused receptionist and we leave the plants in the lunchroom for staff to take home. I suggest that most people wouldn't take the time to do this. This statement makes no sense to her. 'Why would you not?' she asks.

We visit another Delaney + Chin garden, directly across the road from the studio. A year ago, it was a scrap of land covered in junk. Topher and her business partner, Calvin Chin, and their friends cleaned it up. 'We planted it, we paid for the plants and we take care of it.' It's a happy and inviting space, full of texture, colour and life. A hummingbird drinks the nectar of a salvia and a mix of daffodils, daisies and other flowers fill the garden beds. Topher and her team have dramatically transformed the space.

'At lunchtime, all the hospital workers come here. I ask them why they come when they can sit over there at the hospital. They say, "That's landscape, this is a garden". These are not people who are aficionados. They don't even blink when they say it. They like it here because there are flowers and it's a garden. Every single seat is taken. People walk by, they stop and touch things, they look at it. No one knows we clean up this place every day. They're just happy. They sit here, not afraid of anything. There was a school science class here yesterday. Yet this garden wasn't here a year ago.'

It's not the big stuff that counts, according to Topher. 'Life is a series of iterative experiences. Little things happen. If you love someone, it's how they smile or how they look at you. You remember that for life. This garden, it's a little thing. It's what we all can do.'

'Action, intention, attention. It's a motto' she says, as she strides across the road to her studio. On the way she stops to chat with a woman who is holding a stop sign for a road construction company. Topher gave her a rose from the garden the day before. Today the woman has brought flowers from her home garden with the hope that Topher can arrange them for her – she wants to give them to her mother. Of course Topher will. 'If I didn't have the garden I never would have met her. Why not give her a rose, right? There'll be more. She's now got a friend. Things change.'

I ask Topher if she was always good at acting with intention and attention. She wasn't. 'After I had cancer, that's when I changed. I realised that this is it. It's not a dress rehearsal. Care and action are two different things. You gotta act.'

TOPHER DELANEY ON TRANSFORMATION, FAITH AND DAFFODILS

On transformation

I was diagnosed with breast cancer when I was thirty-nine. I went to the doctor on a Tuesday night and he said, 'Tomorrow, full mastectomy surgery'. I said, 'Wow, wait, give me a day or something.' He told me to go think about it. I asked him where the sanctuary was. He said, 'What sanctuary? What are you talking about?' I said, 'You know, the place you go to think about things because you're going to die.' He told me to go to the cafeteria.

In the cafeteria there was a basketball game on the television and a man eating Cheetos in the booth next to me. I thought, 'This is unbelievable.' I looked at the game, I looked at the guy and I just said, 'God, if you can get me out of this, I'll do everything in the rest of my life to do work in transformation. I'll work for people, I'll change my whole attitude, I'll get rid of the BMW, I'm done.' I created my first hospital garden a month later.

On faith

Gardening is not just about making places that are pretty, although that's a great thing. It's about making sure that we are testaments of belief, and that we are acting as testaments of faith in the future. You can't make a garden without faith. Gardening is a faith-based practice. This worries a lot of people when they hear it, but there's nothing wrong with that.

On landscape architecture

Landscape architecture has taken a very bad turn. Before, you needed to know plants, you needed to know how things worked. Not anymore. We're going to hell in a handbasket and you don't want to teach people plants? You don't want to teach people how to know what's around them? What is it that you want to teach them? What could you possibly want people to know? How to do a CAD drawing? That's not going to save you.

On daffodils

I love daffodils, they're my saviours, so I plant them.

IDEAS OF BEAUTY

Rental decadence

DAVID WHITWORTH

DAVID WHITWORTH, LANDSCAPE ARCHITECT AND PAINTER,
IS A THOUGHTFUL MAN WITH A DEEP APPRECIATION FOR
BEAUTY. FOR HIM, BEAUTY IS NOT A SUPERFICIAL PURSUIT.
IT IS A POWERFUL FORCE THAT STIMULATES IMAGINATION AND
CREATIVITY. 'BEAUTY DOES NOT LINGER; IT ONLY VISITS,' WROTE
IRISH POET AND PHILOSOPHER JOHN O'DONOHUE. 'YET BEAUTY'S
VISITATION AFFECTS US AND INVITES US INTO ITS RHYTHM;
IT CALLS US TO FEEL, THINK AND ACT BEAUTIFULLY IN THE
WORLD ... A LIFE WITHOUT DELIGHT IS ONLY HALF A LIFE.'
DAVID KNOWS THIS INSTINCTIVELY.

COLOUR REFERENCE: TASSEL FERN (*Huperzia squarrosa*)   LOCATION: CHIPPENDALE, AUSTRALIA

IDEAS OF BEAUTY

'I consider beauty as something much broader than just pleasing arrangements. I think of beautiful gardens as places that inspire and then reward my curiosity.' David Whitworth's description of beauty in relation to gardens is pretty much the way I'd describe David himself.

David is a gentle and intelligent man, with a dry sense of humour and an incredible aesthetic. He sticks out from the crowd – not in a 'look at me' way, more in a 'this is me' way. I didn't need to see David's garden to know it was fabulous. Soon after we met, I invited myself over.

David and I share an affinity for beauty, gardens, poetry and stuffing tiny rental courtyards with plants. 'I'm like one of those ladies who ends up with a house full of frog ornaments. Everyone knows she has a soft spot for frogs, so they keep giving them to her. That's what's happened with me. I don't ever say no to plants. I just say, "Sure, I'll find space".'

David's backyard belongs to a rambling, old inner-city terrace house that he rents with three flatmates. Over the last ten years he has slowly transformed the small rear courtyard from a 'run-down, mosquito-ridden mud puddle' to a lush and leafy jungle. 'We had a chook run to begin with, and then we tried growing vegetables but it was too shady.'

The most recent incarnation of the garden began in 2012, after David started studying landscape architecture. Slowly but surely, he evicted the mosquitoes, removed the clotheslines that criss-crossed the walkway, and covered the slimy paving with timber decking tiles. He built a raised deck using scavenged timber boards and old pallets, and began to fill the space with plants.

It's a one-of-every-plant kind of garden. The sort we were advised against creating at design school (the rules: plants should be in clumps of three or more, and less is more). Yet David's garden, with a Japanese maple (*Acer palmatum*) elbowing a bird of paradise (*Strelitzia nicolai*), a rubber plant *(Ficus elastica* 'Rubra') dancing with a euphorbia (*Euphorbia tirucalli*), a monstera *(Monstera deliciosa)* lurching up one wall and a tea tree (*Leptospermum* spp.) screening the other, and masses of pots all filled with special little specimen plants, is gorgeous. It breaks the rules beautifully.

David's plant acquisition strategy is simple. 'I either request plants for my birthday, or I give them to myself as a reward. I once finished a shitty exam and I was like, "Right, I need a $300 *Ficus lyrata* right NOW!"'

David loves working in his garden, not sitting in it. 'In a way, gardeners are always building to a point that never arrives. I often think I'll fix something and then just sit back, have a cup of tea and enjoy it, but it doesn't happen. I've realised I prefer the rearranging, the tending, the watering. I think "to tend" is my favourite verb. It implies that you are creative, or nurturing, but almost invisibly so. It's also aspirational. To tend is to sustain a state of caring. It is a state I'd like to aim for in more areas of my life than just gardening.'

As the gardener tends to the garden, the garden nurtures the gardener. It's a space that teaches patience, perspective and connection. 'I like that my plants don't share my worries. The leaves don't fall off my maple if I've had a bad day, which is a nice way to be reminded that I'm a tiny part of a bigger system. Gardening gives me quiet time to sit with my thoughts and let them evaporate or get closer to resolution.'

As well as being a place of action and contemplation, David's garden is an expression of his ideas of beauty. Plants take centre stage. David uses them to create rooms, microclimates and, most importantly, atmosphere.

It's in this space – somewhere between the physicality of a garden and its intangible essence – that David finds beauty. 'Often when I find a garden beautiful, it's the imperceptible, immaterial elements that make it sing – a quality of light, or the sound of certain plants in the wind, or a scent. That's the magic of gardening. It's almost like film-making – it's a complete, holistic and experiential art form.'

Where to next for the man with the fullest and most magical garden in town? 'I'm daydreaming of building a suspended bird's nest–style garden. I've got to go up, because I've run out of space on the ground.'

A grand garden legacy

BEVERLEY MCCONNELL

BEVERLEY MCCONNELL IS THE WOMAN BEHIND ONE OF NEW
ZEALAND'S MOST FAMOUS GARDENS, AYRLIES. A DAB HAND WITH
A GARDEN FORK, AND AN INCREDIBLY PASSIONATE PLANTSWOMAN,
BEVERLEY HAS DEDICATED MUCH OF HER LIFE TO TRANSFORMING
AN EMPTY PADDOCK INTO A LUSH, PAINTERLY WONDERLAND.
DESPITE HAVING RECEIVED NATIONAL AND INTERNATIONAL
RECOGNITION (INCLUDING A NEW ZEALAND ORDER OF MERIT
AND A VEITCH MEMORIAL MEDAL FROM THE ROYAL HORTICULTURAL
SOCIETY) SHE HOLDS NO AIRS AND GRACES. SHE JUST WANTS
TO GARDEN.

COLOUR REFERENCE: CREPE MYRTLE (*Lagerstroemia indica*)   LOCATION: WHITFORD, NEW ZEALAND

Beverley McConnell, or Bev as everyone calls her, is prepared for our visit.
She leads us from the back door of her home, followed by two terriers,
to a seat next to the pool. In her hand are a pair of secateurs. 'I never go
anywhere without them.'

I've been told about Bev by many people. More than one suggested she's
a national treasure. I can see why. Ayrlies, her sixteen-acre, internationally
renowned masterpiece of a garden, is incredible and Bev herself is
instantly engaging. Warmth spills from her eyes and her hands speak
of a lifetime in the garden.

Bev and her husband Malcolm bought this land at Whitford, east
of Auckland, in 1964. A life in the country was one of her very strict
prerequisites for marriage. 'I told him, "I'll only marry you if you don't take
me to the city".' Ayrlies, named after Malcolm's family farm in Scotland,
was paddocks when they first moved in. Malcolm fenced off three acres
around the house for Bev to create a garden. 'I thought that was enough
to begin with. In fact, I thought it would always be enough!'

A trip to England in 1974 changed the garden's course dramatically. While
there, they hired gardener Oliver Briers (who is still pottering in the garden
despite having retired five times!), and Malcolm got very excited about
water. He and Bev were visiting the gardens of Hampton Court Palace,
with its grand lakes and canals and, all of a sudden, Malcolm went very
quiet. 'When I asked him what was wrong, he said, "There's no reason
why you can't have water in your garden". When we got home, he made
arrangements.' A year or so later the garden had grown from three acres
to fifteen, complete with extensive ponds, streams and waterfalls.' Ollie
and I took one look at it said, "What can we do about this?"'

Bev studied art at Canterbury University. 'My father was dying for me to
study art. His mother was a very capable artist. I could never have been
the artist that she was but it was quite useful for the garden.' Her trained
eye guided the evolution of the rapidly growing garden. She was not,
however, issuing orders from the balcony. Quite the opposite — Bev had
as much dirt under her nails as Ollie. 'I was young, I was physically strong,
I could throw rocks around, it wasn't a problem. You have to be strong to
build a garden like this, and also very, very dedicated. And you definitely
need to be a bit mad.'

Ayrlies is an incredible garden. Native plants frame a gravel path
leading from the garden's entrance to a large pond fringed by a curtain
of liquidambar trees (*Liquidambar styraciflua*). The water is black and

glassy and there's a palpable air of mystery and intrigue. It's mesmerising – I find myself walking slower and slower, looking and feeling and looking some more. I breathe the garden in.

Huge expanses of lawn punctuated by grand old trees connect the dark beauty of the pond with the colourful planting around the house. 'The artistry of putting plants together – that's what I love so much. I love looking at all the different textures and colours. I look at something and think, "Oops, I think we need ferns there, because it's gotten a bit bromeliad-looking". Garden pictures grow and they need constant refurbishing, they never stay the same.'

At a time when women (particularly those with five children) were expected to be tethered to the kitchen sink and laundry tub, Bev was lugging stones, planting thousands of trees and contemplating colour and composition in her ever-expanding dream garden, supported by Ollie 'the other man in my life' – and Malcolm. 'Malcolm supported me but he didn't interfere too much. He wrote the cheques, and gardens eat money. He knew that he'd be away a lot and it was very important to have a happy wife. He wasn't silly. I wandered off into the garden a lot, but the children tell me they didn't suffer.'

They mustn't have, because they all want to keep Ayrlies thriving into the future. 'I wrote to all five children and said I'd been so fortunate to have a dream and to be backed by their father to work on my dream. I told them I didn't want to burden them with my dreams, because they were mine, not theirs. Each one wrote back, beautiful letters, saying,"Mum, it's much more than that, it's our heritage and we want to keep it".'

I join Bev and Ollie and the rest of the garden staff at smoko, a daily morning tea and work meeting on the patio of the house. The team's affection for Bev is clear. No-one ever wants to leave. 'Bev works too hard. But she loves what she does, she loves every single plant in the garden,' says Jackie, who helps Bev in the house. Working at Ayrlies is 'a labour of love,' adds Ollie. Though, like all good work relationships, there's room for discussion. 'We've had ding-dongs at times. I used to build the things and Bev used to cover them up.'

Ayrlies is everything to Bev. It's a landscape she's poured her heart, soul and sweat into over the last fifty years. Her love, care and spirit speak through the plants. 'It's a very nourishing place. Visitors sometimes arrive looking a bit stressed, but leave having relaxed and restored their soul a bit. That's really what gardening is about – restoring the soul. Gardeners are the luckiest people.'

As I leave, we wander past a planting bed near the house. 'I haven't quite finished this bit yet,' Bev says. 'I dug out all the grasses but an hour, maybe two, of digging, that's about all I can do.' We talk about her plans for the space and she tells me she's yet to convince her team of her ideas. 'I'm not sure that anybody agrees with me but I'm going to have my way.' And she will. You can't keep a good gardener down.

Heirloom seed hero

CLIVE BLAZEY

CLIVE BLAZEY IS ONE OF THE GREAT VISIONARIES OF AUSTRALIAN GARDENING. HE AND HIS WIFE, PENNY, FOUNDED THE DIGGERS CLUB IN 1978 TO RESCUE AND REINTRODUCE HEIRLOOM SEED VARIETIES, LEADING THE CHARGE AGAINST GENETICALLY MODIFIED AND HYBRIDISED FOOD PLANTS. FORTY YEARS LATER, CLIVE'S DETERMINATION HASN'T WAVERED. HE IS STILL FIGHTING THE GOOD FIGHT FOR DIVERSITY, CLIMATIC SUITABILITY, PRODUCTIVITY AND BEAUTY IN GARDENS.

COLOUR REFERENCE: FOXGLOVE (*Digitalis* 'Glittering Prizes')   LOCATION: NORTHCOTE, AUSTRALIA

Clive Blazey has a reputation. Not only is he an heirloom seed hero and a passionate plantsman with a deep appreciation for beauty, he is a man with strong opinions. He writes books with titles like *There is No Excuse for Ugliness*, says things like, 'I think suburban gardens are almost universally horrible', and irritates people with his stance on eucalyptus trees. 'They're really lousy shade trees.'

When I arrive at his home late one afternoon, the door is wide open and the front yard is an abundant tangle of early-autumn beauty. Low perennial plants like *wormwood* (*Artemisia ludoviciana* 'Valerie Finnis') and cranesbill (*Geranium* x *himalayense* 'Rozanne') spill out onto a gravel and bluestone pathway and echinacea flowers lean towards the end of their lives amid a jungle of wild foliage. 'I'm not a tidy gardener,' Clive says as he ambles up, barefoot, and offers us a drink. We sit on the front verandah of the home he shares with Penny, his wife, and meander verbally around his garden.

Clive has been gardening ideas and plants for most of his life. He and Penny founded mail order seed business The Diggers Club while he was studying business at university. 'I went into Melbourne's Royal Botanic Gardens when I was twenty-two and thought, "That's where I want to live. In a little cottage surrounded by beautiful plants." I suppose everyone has this vision of creating their own little piece of paradise.'

Clive's idea of paradise was plant-based, but it soon became political. The Diggers Club was originally set up to rescue old and interesting varieties of vegetables, but a trip to Iowa in 1991 to visit Kent and Diane Whealy at the Seed Savers Exchange opened Clive's eyes to the importance of preserving heirloom seeds. 'After realising that around ninety-seven per cent of the vegetables grown in the USA in 1900 had been lost, Kent and Diane set about collecting and preserving their seed inheritance. Today, they have saved 20,000 different vegetable varieties and their exchange network keeps these varieties alive.'

In line with his focus on preserving diversity, Clive is a strong opponent of the genetic modification and corporatisation of seeds. 'The greatest threat to plant diversity is the granting of seed patents to multinational chemical and seed companies. Before genetically modified (GM) crops were introduced and patented, around sixty per cent of seeds were publicly owned. Now the ownership of about seventy per cent of the world's seeds is held by just six companies. Gene splicing under a microscope to manipulate ownership and control of seeds for profit is a symptom of how arrogant and separated we have become from nature. No species that loses control of its food supply has ever survived.'

Seed saving is a practice that gardeners and farmers have undertaken for aeons. Saving seeds from one season's crop and replanting them the following year encourages genetic diversity and results in food crops that are best suited to local conditions. A handful of heirloom vegetable seeds weaves a story of people and place over hundreds, even thousands, of years. Seeds mean sustenance, story, shelter. Seed corporatisation undermines this ancient practice and transforms a birthright, story and legacy into private property.

If botanical diversity is the one arm of The Diggers Club, beauty is another. Clive is passionate about the creation of beauty through gardening. His love affair began, of course, with seeds. 'It was from my passion for seeds that my love of creating beauty in the garden began to germinate. Gardening connects you to biology, archaeology and the environment – it offers a fascinating perspective. With gardening, you never get to the stage of being confident you know enough.'

The gardens owned by The Diggers Club – Heronswood and St Erth – are where Clive's focus on seeds, biodiversity, organic gardening principles and beauty combine. The gardens at both properties are incredible – big, rambling, romantic spaces, full of weird and wonderful edible and ornamental plants. Both gardens are a labour of love for Clive, but he no longer works in them. 'When Diggers was a straggling little operation, I'd work all weekend in the garden because we couldn't afford enough gardeners.' As the business expanded they began hiring professionals. A few years ago, Clive was kicked out of the gardening team. 'My staff told me to get out of the garden because I'm not tidy enough for them!'

Clive and Penny recently moved back to the inner city. One of the reasons was that Clive 'wanted to get back into gardening'. Their new home is a generous old beauty built in the 1880s and Clive is in the process of engulfing it in plants. There's an informal perennial garden out the front, a mixture of edible and ornamental plants lining the wide pathway up the side, and a testing ground out the back where he is currently experimenting with different varieties of ferns and bamboo for possible inclusion in The Diggers Club's plant catalogue.

He's clearly relishing the opportunity to have his hands in the dirt again, making as much mess as he wants. 'I'll cut it back in May, do some more weeding, mulch it and that's about it. Apart from fixing the mistakes I've made. I'll have to correct a few of those.'

He's done a great job. The garden is only a year old but it already feels settled and full. He credits the vigorous growth to a truckload of 'zoo poo' fertiliser added to the soil prior to planting. Clive's kids, however, are tougher on him. 'My kids are appalled at my sense of colour. To them it's boring and old-fashioned. They're into pinks and oranges together and stuff like that. I can't see that in a pleasing way at all. This is all a bit ho-hum for them, I think.' The colour palette is a mix of grey, blue and mauve tones — not avant-garde enough for his children, perhaps, but cohesive and beautiful nonetheless.

His children may not approve of Clive's use of colour in the garden but they certainly appreciate the food he produces. His children and grandchildren regularly eat tomatoes, silverbeet and self-sown potatoes from his backyard. Just don't ask him to cook. Given his thirty-year association with edible plants, organic gardening and heritage seeds, you might assume that Clive is a foodie. He's not. Absolutely not. 'If I ever offer to cook for my kids, they say, "Don't, Dad". I'm a so-called food legend because of the work we did with growing heritage plants, not because I know how to cook them.'

Clive Blazey is a surprising character. He's a big personality, a passionate gardener, and a visionary whose actions have changed the course of gardening like few others. While his ideas can be divisive, they come from a place of truth. His desire for change, his concern for the environment and his love of beauty and cohesion underpin his actions. In this sense, Clive is an artist and plants are his medium. 'I'm really fascinated by plants and I'm optimistic enough to think that I can get it right, eventually.'

AND

ORDER

CHAOS

Dahlias, dirty nails and

LUCY CULLITON

LUCY CULLITON WAS BORN WITH DIRT UNDER HER FINGERNAILS.
A HIGHLY ACCLAIMED ARTIST, KEEN GARDENER AND ANIMAL
RESCUER, LUCY IS HAPPIEST WHEN CREATING IN HER STUDIO
OR GARDEN – DOG, BIRD, GOAT OR HORSE BY HER SIDE. SHE'S
A WOMAN VERY MUCH OF THE EARTH (WITH A SOFT SPOT FOR
DAHLIAS).

COLOUR REFERENCE: DAHLIA (*Dahlia* spp.)   LOCATION: BIBBENLUKE, AUSTRALIA

glorious disorder

ORDER AND CHAOS

Bibbenluke Lodge, a gorgeous old property nestled into the side of a hill, is where Lucy Culliton lives, paints and gardens. The driveway is lined with pine trees and leads to a 1930s homestead and outbuildings, a big wild garden and a few acres of paddocks. As well as Lucy and her partner, Jamie, this is also home to what can only be described as a menagerie. It's a bit of a moveable feast, but her best guess is that it currently consists of three cows, a few horses, forty sheep, a couple of goats, two pigs, two emus, a shed full of pigeons, some galahs, chickens, a magpie and four dogs.

It's an enchanting place and Lucy is an incredibly relaxed, no-nonsense host. She takes us on a wander around the garden and we discuss her various horticultural enterprises. Like how she's going to remove the English elm suckers between the road and her house and replace them with masses of rhododendrons. 'When people drive along the road and see them in flower they'll go, "What the fuck?" That's what I want.'

There was plenty in the garden to begin with, but she likes to add to what's already there. She's learning what works and what doesn't. 'When I first came here I tried anything that said cold climate on the label. They'd die, die, die. I just keep doing things like lupins and dahlias because they work.'

Bibbenluke Lodge is her first large garden, but Lucy is no stranger to plants. Before this, she lived in the inner-city Sydney suburb of Surry Hills. That garden was all about succulents – she became a member of the Cactus and Succulent Society of NSW and devoted herself to painting her collection. Next was the village of Hartley, west of the Blue Mountains, where her focus was cactus and another collection of works inspired by her plants. She's now painted the flowers at Bibbenluke, the weeds of the Monaro, the interiors of her house and, most recently, a series of sixty portraits of the animals under her care called *The Residents of Bibbenluke Lodge*.

'I like nurturing,' Lucy tells me when I ask her what draws her to gardening. This is clear, but it's also clear she likes hard work. She gets up early to feed the animals and then heads to her studio to work on her upcoming exhibition before doing more farm jobs in the afternoon. As well as being labour-intensive, the garden nurtures Lucy and her art practice as much as she nurtures it. 'Gardening is a mental exercise which is different to painting. It's something that's never finished and I never intend it to be finished. It's hard work but it pays off – I think it just suits me.'

To say Lucy's garden is all about dahlias would be an overstatement. It does seem, however, that they may be her latest obsession. There's certainly a dahlia hierarchy happening – the common self-seeders live down the bottom of the garden, sharing a bed with a wild pumpkin vine. The show ponies are closer to the house, planted in beds near the front door where she can keep a close eye on them and keep them staked and well-watered.

Her attention has paid off. 'Lucy has won plenty of prizes for her art,' Jamie says, 'but I don't think I've ever seen her happier than at the Bombala Show last week, winning prizes for her dahlias.'

Lucy's garden is wild and abundant. It's a space to meander through slowly, offering incredibly beautiful vignettes on both macro and micro levels. It's also, most importantly, a window into her world. 'I only do it for myself. Every gardener only ever does it for themselves.'

This is where the beauty and power of gardening can be found. Gardens are expressions, not exhibits. They only have to suit the hand that nurtures them, and if they do, nothing more needs to be said.

DAHLIAS, DIRTY NAILS AND GLORIOUS DISORDER

ORDER AND CHAOS

DAHLIAS, DIRTY NAILS AND GLORIOUS DISORDER

Punk landscape archite

DAVID GODSHALL

A SELF-DESCRIBED 'GROWN UP PUNK WITH CONTROL ISSUES',
DAVID GODSHALL IS A LANDSCAPE ARCHITECT AND CO-OWNER OF
TERREMOTO, A LANDSCAPE ARCHITECTURE FIRM WITH OFFICES
IN LOS ANGELES AND SAN FRANCISCO. WITH HIS PARTICULAR
BLEND OF IRREVERENCE, CREATIVITY AND INTELLIGENCE, DAVID
GODSHALL IS LEADING A NEW WAVE OF GARDEN-MAKING – NOT
ONLY CREATING SPACES THAT ARE CONCEPTUALLY EXCITING,
RULE BREAKING AND ATMOSPHERIC, BUT ALSO REDEFINING
WHAT A GARDEN IS.

ORDER AND CHAOS

David Godshall and I are plant penpals. He occasionally writes stories for *The Planthunter* online magazine with titles like 'Landscape maintenance and fear of death' and 'Garden anarchy in LA.' His approach to garden-making and garden-thinking is both avant-garde and soulful. 'Gardening satisfies the impulse and need for awe, gratefulness, empathy and love in a way nothing else can.'

David and his business partner, Alain Peauroi, started Terremoto in 2013. Six years later, with a staff of nine, the Terremoto team continually push horticultural, conceptual and material boundaries. Their output – a raft of eclectic, immersive and surprising garden design and art projects – stands in stark contrast to the sameness and sterility of many design portfolios. While their gardens don't have a particular aesthetic stamp or adhere to a certain style, there's always a story running through the soil of each space. 'A successful Terremoto project in some way contributes to cultural conversations, but the theme of the conversation changes from project to project.'

'We started our office because we believe there's a glaring void in the US for landscape architectural work that has a conceptual or intellectual basis. It sounds fancy but it's not. The way we apply materials, horticulture, and geometry (or lack thereof) to a site should be guided by a grounding concept that we can push back on as we design and build.' For example, in one project David and his team might play around with horticultural conventions – mixing plants with different meanings and symbology to energise a space, provoke conversation and thought. In another, 'maybe a small budget has driven us to build the entire project from two-inch by four-inch pieces of wood and we're pushing that unit as far as we can take it.'

David's Echo Park studio in LA is surrounded by a street garden consisting of a mashup of Californian natives like white sage (*Salvia apiana*), imports like rockrose (*Cistus* spp.) and tough guys like prickly pear (*Opuntia ficus-indica*) and agave (*Agave attenuata*). Big chunks of wood are used as seats and a mural stating 'what we do is secret' adorns the building's wall.

We jump into David's car, and he takes us on a tour of some of Terremoto's local garden projects. Our first stop is not a project. It's a pile of concrete boulders in a car park on top of a hill in Elysian Park – according to David, it's an impromptu Zen garden of the Anthropocene. He explains, 'Take Ryōan-ji, the prototypical Japanese Zen garden, for example. First of all, as a Westerner and non-Buddhist, I can't really understand it. But – to be an arrogant Western male and postulate like I understand it – I would suggest that one reading is that it's a metaphorically heavy rumination on life, entropy, understanding and maintenance.'

He points to three chunks of concrete, rock and rubble. 'These are the boulders of the Anthropocene. As the city cannibalises itself in the name of progress, it devours and regurgitates itself constantly. These are the physical manifestations of this. Within this concrete fuselage, one can connect to notions of urban entropy, life and death.' Notions of what a garden is and can be are discussed in the front seats of the car as we wind down the hill. 'The world is a garden!' says David with glee.

Our tour continues as David zips us around the streets of east LA. We visit a tiny garden constructed predominantly of buckets (they're used for planters, seats, tables and more); a residential garden with pink walls, a cactus collection and a series of symbolic trees; a garden ruin on top of a hill looking out over Silver Lake Reservoir – a new dream project for David and his team – and finally, David's home garden perched on the top of a ridge in Echo Park. He lives here with his wife, Lauren Jordan, their son, Wolfgang, and dog, Momo.

David's garden is, as expected, curious and gorgeous. Wide concrete steps lead through a wild street planting featuring a mix of cactus, succulents like echeveria and century plant and the grey foliage of sagebrush (*Artemisia californica*). A big old jacaranda (*Jacaranda mimosifolia*) frames the entry to the property and a low, timber fence with diagonal panels separates the garden from the street. A tangle of foliage greets us as we walk through the gate. The structure is simple and raw, and the plants are free to do as they wish. It wasn't always like this. David and Lauren started off with a vision of a native Californian plant palette. 'Plants that evolved in southern California are acclimatised to suffering, drought and heat. They want nothing to do with an annoyingly regular irrigation system, don't like high-quality topsoil, are viciously seasonal and often short-lived. We planted natives and killed most of them. Then we learned to neglect our garden and it began to thrive. We kept at it until our garden grew into its current state of total punk-rock anarchy.'

Nowadays the garden 'exists in an interesting middle ground of self-seeding revolution'. Things come and go as they please, natives fight with edibles, Wolfgang plays in the undergrowth and birds chase bugs. It's a vibrant, well-loved space. 'My garden is more or less indicative of who I am as a human being. A grown-up punk with control issues.'

David and I sit in his wild garden as the sun retreats and talk about the future of garden-making. We decide it has to be raucous and fun and rule-bending. A garden can be a pile of rocks on a hill, three plants growing out of a crack in the pavement, or a narrow timber path zigzagging through a forest. It's simply a matter of perception. The more we expand our ideas of what a garden is and can be, the more opportunities there are for seeing the garden as a place of meaning and cultural value, of conversation – a place where humans can converse with our inner and outer wilderness.

For David the garden of the future is 'a little messy and wild, but it's radical'.

PUNK LANDSCAPE ARCHITECTURE IN LA

ORDER AND CHAOS

PUNK LANDSCAPE ARCHITECTURE IN LA

A landscape of the soul

TRISHA DIXON

TRISHA DIXON IMMERSES HERSELF FULLY IN LIFE. SHE'S AN
ADVENTURER, TRAVELLER, THINKER AND GARDENER AND SPENDS
MONTHS AT A TIME AWAY FROM HER FARM. YET, THE LANDSCAPE
AND GARDEN SURROUNDING HER HOME IS AN INTEGRAL PART OF
THE FABRIC OF HER BEING, GROUNDING HER IN A WAY ONLY
A LANDSCAPE OF THE SOUL CAN. TRISHA'S IS A STORY ABOUT
THE NOURISHMENT THAT COMES FROM A DEEP CONNECTION
TO PLACE AND AN OPEN-HEARTED DIALOGUE WITH NATURE.

COLOUR REFERENCE: JAPANESE WISTERIA (*Wisteria floribunda*)   LOCATION: BOBUNDARA, AUSTRALIA

ORDER AND CHAOS

A LANDSCAPE OF THE SOUL

ORDER AND CHAOS

To get to Trisha Dixon's farm, we have to drive through a maze of narrow dirt roads punctuated by the spotlit dashes of startled kangaroos, potholes and a very occasional driveway. It's dark, the phone reception is non-existent and there's talk of being lost and having to spend the night in the back of the van, but the directions she gave us to her property, Bobundara, lead us to the right place eventually. We arrive to the welcoming sound of classical music blasting from the homestead, which is nestled deep in the embrace of the dark landscape. Trisha bounds out of the house to greet us, and she's an incredibly welcome sight. We share a meal before heading to bed.

I'm always excited to wake somewhere new after arriving at night. Seeing the landscape, not just feeling its form in the dark, gets me out of bed early, eager to find out exactly where I am. I watch the magical Bobundara landscape awake, coffee in hand, as the sun rises over a low hill to the east.

Bobundara is nestled in a fold of the vast, rolling forms of the Monaro countryside in southern New South Wales. The garden is protected and green and bordered by a small creek. The surrounding landscape, however, is vast, vast, vast. With treeless rolling hills, huge skies and occasional stands of twisted snow gums, it's expansive in summer and harsh in winter.

Trisha has lived here since the mid-1980s. When she first saw it, the house reminded her of her childhood home. She loved it immediately. 'It was a funny old house. It was a bit shambolic, but had integrity and a great atmosphere.'

The oldest parts of the house were built in 1831, when the property was one of Monaro's major pastoral holdings. The garden is historically significant. It is described in the NSW State Heritage Register as 'extensive pleasure gardens which have retained their original 19th century cottage garden character'.

The bones of the garden remain, and Trisha respects them deeply. Rather than being clipped and controlled, as they might have been in the past, they've been allowed to soften with age and are cloaked with a looseness of foliage and form. Borders are a tangle of green, wisteria creeps hopefully across the verandah, and a thicket of elms, heavy with magic and mystery, stands at the end of the garden. A creek, which for many years was excluded from the garden by a fence, winds its way around the space. The garden bleeds into the landscape, stewarded by Trisha, who both nurtures and is nurtured by the land at Bobundara.

'My mother just loved gardening. Dad used to say that if he wasn't there, she'd forget about eating – she'd just get lost in the garden all day.' A childhood spent in a garden often leads to a life in a garden, and Trisha is no exception. An author and photographer, she's written and contributed to many books about gardens and landscapes. Nowadays, she wanders the globe leading tours focusing on gardens, art, literature and landscape.

Trisha came to gardens via aviation. In her early twenties, she decided studying science at university wasn't for her. 'I was staying with a friend who was working for a man who needed a pilot, so I became a pilot,' she says matter-of-factly. 'I told my parents and they said, "But darling, you can't fly". I learnt very quickly. That was that.'

While she was learning to fly, Trisha worked in the ABC newsroom in Canberra. 'I'd work all night and fly all day. It was just the best.' After a few years of flying, she returned to the ABC to work as a weather presenter. From there, she moved to Sydney to work for a newspaper, got married and moved south to Bobundara.

Living in a historic house surrounded by a historic garden, Trisha's attention soon turned to the garden. 'When we first moved here, there were the beautiful big old trees and lots of fruit trees, which was really lovely. But then there were these conifers, modern roses and marigolds. It had no soul. I tried to put the mystery back into the garden, and to open it up to include the landscape surrounding it.'

Trisha's two main design influences were Irish gardener William Robinson, and Australian garden designer Edna Walling. 'I was always going to go a little bit wild! I like axis and form but I love softness. Robinson and Walling both had very architectural gardens, but they were always offset by a wild garden that wasn't watered and barely mowed. It made its own beauty. That's what I wanted.'

Bobundara is a magical garden – it's atmospheric and soulful. Trisha's influence is shown not by what's been planted, pruned or controlled, but by what's been left alone and allowed to be itself. It demonstrates a deep sensitivity and respect for the place, the landscape and its history. It's also a practical measure. 'If my garden reflects me, then I'm a very, very messy person. If I wanted it to be perfect I'd have to be here every day of the year, working on it. Instead, I choose to have an exciting life of people, photography, travel, art and family. You've got to decide what's important to you. I just love the whole adventure of life.'

Trisha is one of life's great enthusiasts. Her enthusiasm and energy, and the joy she seems to find abounding everywhere around her, is contagious. 'When I arrive home after being away my heart sings. I'm like a child. I skip around the house and garden. I have the music going so loud that when I bicycle out to get the mail, even at the front gate, I can still hear it.'

The poetic meanderings of Leonard Cohen's final album, *You Want It Darker*, accompany us as we photograph Trisha's garden, chasing the morning light. We leave reluctantly. The wild maze of roads we were engulfed by on the way in is nowhere to be seen.

Welcome to Cevanland

CEVAN FORRISTT

SILICON VALLEY – INTERNATIONAL HUB OF TECHNOLOGY
COMPANIES, DIGITAL ENTREPRENEURS AND VENTURE CAPITALISTS
– HARDLY SEEMS LIKE THE PLACE TO FIND SOMEONE LIKE CEVAN
FORRISTT. HE IS A BRILLIANTLY MAD LANDSCAPE DESIGNER,
ARTIST AND MAGICIAN WITH AN INCREDIBLY CREATIVE GARDEN.
VISITING IT IS LIKE STEPPING INTO ANOTHER WORLD.

COLOUR REFERENCE: GIANT TIMBER BAMBOO (*Phyllostachys bambusoides*)   LOCATION: SAN JOSE, USA

a

ORDER AND CHAOS

ORDER AND CHAOS

A visit to Cevan Forristt's garden should require a passport. It's another country, if not another world. As soon as the tall, timber entry gates close on the quiet suburban San Jose street, you cross the border into Cevan's wild, green nation. Lanterns hang from trees, succulents grow out of ancient Chinese horse troughs, and lichen marks walls made of granite blocks reclaimed from local demolition sites. I have never, ever, experienced such an immersive garden. It's an easy place to enter and a hard one to leave.

Cevan (pronounced Kevin) is just like his garden: brilliantly iconoclastic. He opens the front gate wearing only a towel around his waist. Later, when he emerges from among the bamboo in the rear garden, he's wearing a Hawaiian shirt and a green feather toupee. Other outfits appear and disappear over the course of our visit.

Cevan has been pushing boundaries, in and out of the garden, all his life. 'I was an easy kid to raise because they could just put me in the garden and I entertained myself.' As a teenager, he used to 'borrow' plants from gardens in the neighbourhood. 'I once stole a juniper tree from a nearby garden and bonsaied it. After a few years, I got bored and returned it in the middle of the night. Here was a tree that was in the ground in their garden a few years ago and now it was a nice big bonsai in a pot on their porch.' Cevan stopped stealing plants after one of his friend's mothers said, out of the blue, 'Plants have been mysteriously disappearing in the neighbourhood but no-one is going to say anything, yet. If it continues, there'll be a problem.' He got the message.

Plants and gardening were an escape for Cevan during his childhood and teenage years. 'My family was kind of crazy.' He changed his first name from Kevin to Cevan and his last name to Forristt when he was in his early twenties. 'I had a friend who did numerology and we figured out what name would suit me. With a new name, you can reinvent yourself. It worked.'

At university, Cevan meandered between plants and art. He studied ornamental horticulture, ceramics and art, ending up with a degree in art history. 'I studied horticulture, but everyone was so dry. I'm a nerd but I didn't think I could do that my whole life. I'd go to botany classes, then I'd do acting classes. I studied stage set design, archaeology, ceramics and art history. I'd hang out with crazy weirdo people. I like extremes because they're therapeutic.'

Cevan's been designing gardens since the late 1980s – in his own way, of course. 'My gardens can't be drawn up on paper. They're very collaborative – I pull the client into the mix. Often, clients think I'll be difficult to work with because I'm creative but they realise I'm very fluid and easy. I'm open, because my ego is not attached to the job. I only do one job at a time, and I live and breathe that job. I'm a monogamist. When we're done, we get divorced and they pay my final settlement.'

Cevan's garden designs are not restricted to a particular style. 'I'm only limited by your request,' he tells his clients. He's designed gardens for forty-year-old tortoises ('I made friends with them, I'd bring them apples and corn, they loved it'), Mediterannean-style retreats, and he's about to embark on a garden channelling the film *Midnight in the Garden of Good and Evil*.

For Cevan, a garden should be a place of atmosphere and excitement. 'My gardens look like something could happen in them. Most gardens are dead. Nothing can happen in them. I don't care where a rock or tree goes, I'm more interested in what it feels like.' Cevan's aim is to make 'countries' for his clients, based on their personalities, desires and dislikes. 'I get into the psychology of it. I ask people what their fantasy garden is, but then I ask what their nightmare garden is. What I really care about is what they hate about their childhood, their life. Then I know what not to do.'

Cevan's clients love the gardens he creates for them. 'I have a lot of clients who were never into gardening. Now, all they want to do is weed their new garden.' Other clients never want him to leave. 'They say, "You're not going to leave are you? We want you to stay – your energy, your flurry, your everything – you have all this stuff going on".'

Cevan's own garden is a masterpiece. He bought the quarter-acre property in San Jose in 1989 and began working on the garden in the early 1990s. He didn't have a grand plan. 'I'm organic, I just started laying it out and piecing different elements together. I started in the back corner, because everything is so heavy.'

There's an Asian vibe – 'I've been to Thailand at least twenty times' – but, of course, the garden doesn't sit neatly within that category. It consists of stone, stone, stone, bamboo, stone, water, succulent, stone, stone, tree, stone. Buddhas stand next to Ming vessels and columns reclaimed from demolished San Francisco buildings rest on their sides or act as a bases for carved stone lanterns and plants. And there is always more, more, more. Magic, chaos and colour abound. Cevanlandia is an incredibly beautiful and mad world, and it breaks all the rules spectacularly.

Time bends, boundaries warp, people arrive and food is shared in the bamboo-enveloped temple in the rear garden. By the time I leave, it's late. The garden at night is yet another world. Shadows reach in towards the patterns of light dancing on stone paving, and somewhere in the darkness lies the portal to the quiet San Jose street. 'People often can't find their way out. They get pulled into a vacuum.'

I manage to find the gate, and cross the border reluctantly. Street lights, parked cars and the quiet front yards of suburban houses greet me – I'm back in California but I think I'd like to stay in Cevanlandia.

When more is more ind

GAYLENE KRAJEWSKI

GAYLENE KRAJEWSKI'S TINY CITY APARTMENT IS MORE GARDEN
THAN HOUSE. IT'S JAM-PACKED WITH PLANTS AND VINTAGE
PARAPHERNALIA AND REWARDS THE CLOSEST OF OBSERVATION.
IT'S PURE CREATIVE EXPRESSION, FUELLED BY GAYLENE'S DEEP
LOVE OF PLANTS AND EYE FOR DETAIL.

COLOUR REFERENCE: RUBBER PLANT (*Ficus elastica*)   LOCATION: MELBOURNE, AUSTRALIA

It's nine o'clock on a Sunday morning and I am reclining on an antique chaise longue in Gaylene Krajewski's tiny city apartment. I need to rest my eyes for a few minutes after the visual onslaught of my first visit to Gaylene's plant-packed home.

'I'm a maximalist,' she says. She's also a collector. Somehow, she's managed to fit sixty-three plants, numerous ceramic kitchenware sets, record collections, vintage ephemera and more into just seventy square metres. There's not a speck of dust to be found. It's the tiniest, fullest, cleanest space I've ever seen.

Gaylene has loved and lived with plants since she was a child. 'I grew up in the workroom of my mother's flower shop.' Every day after school and during the school holidays, Gaylene helped in her mother's shop. Becoming a florist when she finished high school was a no-brainer. She already was one.

She moved away when she was eighteen and worked as a nanny for six years. When her mother died, Gaylene returned to her home town and floristry. She started her own flower shop when she was twenty-six. But then love called. 'I'd known Johnny since I was twenty. I secretly loved him and he secretly loved me, but we never told each other.' Johnny wrote her a letter declaring his true feelings, and she packed up the shop and left within six months. 'Their wedding was organised around the flowering season of Gaylene's favourite bloom – violets. Gaylene wore a purple velvet dress, a violet-encrusted beret and carried a bouquet of violets.

'I've never consciously thought, "I want to be a florist". It's almost like it's my birthright. I guess it's just who I am,' Gaylene tells me as we explore her space. The plants in her home are a natural extension of her floral beginnings. 'When we moved here ten years ago, I only had one plant, a peace lily (*Spathiphyllum wallisii*), and I didn't even like him. He's over there in the corner, though. I couldn't throw him away.'

From that lone, sad peace lily, Gaylene's collection grew and grew. 'I just started buying a few plants and then a few more. And then my ninety-year-old Aunty Irene started giving me cuttings. Suddenly I've got sixty-three plants!' Irene is responsible for the begonias, the donkey's tails (*Sedum morganianum*), coleus (*Solenostemon*), African violets (*Saintpaulia*) and much more. 'Each plant has a story or some sort of meaning.'

'I have a nodding violet (*Streptocarpus caulescens*) which started as a tiny cutting from Aunty Irene's plant. It now measures one-and-a-half metres long! Aunty Irene grew her plant from a cutting taken from my Aunty Faye's plant in the 1980s. Faye grew hers from a cutting taken from my grandmother's plant in the 1970s. Naturally, this is one of my favourite plants – it's a multi-generational thing. I am going to grow one for my nephew James who has just moved into his own place, so it continues on down the line.'

Then there's the hoya number one. While working at a plant shop, Gaylene discovered that each hoya plant that came into the shop had a number. 'I decided I needed to collect them all, starting at number one. This proved harder than it sounds. After years of looking for a number one, we found it among some new stock in the shop. It was so exciting! It is one of my favourite plants. I always look at it and say "Hello, Hoya Number One".'

But how does she fit all her plants and their stories into her apartment? 'It's like a three-dimensional jigsaw. When I get something new, it takes me ages to figure out how it's going to fit in. I often lie on the bed and just stare out there and figure out how I'm going to make it work.'

And what about repotting, transplanting, dividing – all those plant nurturing jobs that are best done outdoors? Gaylene's got it sorted. 'This whole area becomes a garden,' she says, indicating nearly all of the living room with expansive arm movements. 'I say to Johnny, "You can't walk this way, I'm doing my gardening". From the fruit bowl to the end of the table is the gardening zone.'

Gaylene's plants are some of the happiest I've seen growing indoors. As you might expect, there's a structure to their care routine. 'Sunday is my watering day. I have a proper look at each plant, cut any dead leaves, check whether they've got water in the saucer and give them a big drink if they need it.' The happiest plant is the fiddle leaf fig (*Ficus lyrata*). 'Every morning, we pour half a glass of water on the fig. It gets a little bit of water all the time. Unless there's some in the saucer, then we don't add any.'

It's not all sunshine and rainbows in Gaylene's indoor garden, though. Plants need to pull their weight or they get a serious talking to. Like her maidenhair fern. 'He was not doing well. I cut him back and started again with him many times until one day I said, very firmly, "This is your last chance. If you don't start doing something, this is it. You will be gone." I couldn't believe my eyes the next day when he had poked up a little new healthy green frond! I definitely believe in talking to plants.'

Given Gaylene's love of plants, and fluorescent green thumb, I suspect she'd go wild if she had an outdoor garden. She agrees. There's even a little place with the perfect name – Violet Town. 'I've never even been there, but I've decided that's where we need to go!' I can't imagine letting Gaylene loose on a large suburban lot. I ask her what she'd do if she had more room. 'Oh, I'd fill it,' she says. Of course she would. She's a maximalist at heart.

WHEN MORE IS MORE INDOORS

ORDER AND CHAOS

WHEN MORE IS MORE INDOORS

The plant maestro

SIMON RICKARD

SIMON RICKARD IS A GARDENER AND BAROQUE BASSOONIST.
HE SPLITS HIS TIME BETWEEN PERFORMING MUSIC AND
NURTURING GARDENS, ATTACKING BOTH PURSUITS WITH PASSION,
INTELLIGENCE AND CREATIVITY. SIMON'S BELIEF THAT 'GARDENING
IS THE HIGHEST EXPRESSION OF HUMAN ART' IS CLEARLY
ILLUSTRATED IN HIS HOME GARDEN. IT'S THE WORK OF A MASTER.

COLOUR REFERENCE: NAKED LADY (x *Amarygia*)   LOCATION: TRENTHAM, AUSTRALIA

ORDER AND CHAOS

Simon Rickard didn't want us to photograph his garden on the outskirts of a small country town. He said it was looking tired and worn out at the end of a long, hot summer. We dropped in anyway, 'just to have a quick look', and were stopped in our tracks.

Simon's weatherboard house, painted a rich, dark red, is nestled among exuberant, textural plantings. Tall clumps of silvergrass (*Miscanthus transmorrisonensis*) greet us as they wave in the breeze, royal purple smoke bushes (*Cotinus coggygria* 'Grace') lurch upwards and frame the house, and a series of rare and beautiful low shrubs like Marlborough rock daisy (*Pachystegia insignis*) and varieties of euphorbia line a simple gravel walkway that leads towards a narrow gap in a dark green escallonia hedge. The mystery is intoxicating – I need to see what's on the other side.

Greeting me is one of the most considered and masterful perennial planting designs I've seen in Australia. It is a garden room, enclosed on all four sides by a tall hedge and filled with texture, colour, foliage and form in a way that feels just right. A narrow pathway winds through the space and I find myself walking up and back and up again. Looking, looking, looking. I am almost speechless. The rest of the garden comprises an extensive vegetable garden, lawn areas, Simon's beloved Cayuga ducks and a woodland walk. It's beautifully designed and beautifully tended. Even at its apparent worst, this garden is incredible.

Simon is a fascinating and highly intelligent man who has been obsessed with plants from a very young age. He was one of the founding members of the Canberra Orchid Society, way back in the 1980s when he was just twelve years old. He credits his grandmother, and Kmart, for nurturing his plant love. 'Whenever I went to visit my nan, I'd be handed a pair of secateurs and given free rein in the garden to go and pick Mum a bunch of flowers, eat strawberries or pick apples.' And Kmart is where his orchidelirium began. 'I saw a native orchid in Kmart one day and nagged my parents to buy it, which they did. It started my whole collection.'

Over his teenage years Simon amassed a collection of around a hundred orchid plants. 'Back then, orchids were quite rare. I'd write away for a catalogue, receive it, then write back with my order and money stuck to the letter.'

Although originally committed to the idea of studying botany or horticulture at university, work experience at the Australian National Botanic Gardens changed his mind. 'It left me cold, which was weird because I loved plants.' He decided to pursue his other love, music, and studied at the Canberra School of Music before heading to the Netherlands for three years of postgraduate study.

When he left Australia, he bequeathed his orchid collection to his parents. 'Mum and Dad still send me photos of them on the dining room table.' After six years overseas, he returned home to lecture in music history at the Australian National University. Three years of temporary employment contracts got the better of his sanity, so he decided to 'mow lawns and cut hedges' for a living instead, 'because at least I know where my next job is coming from'.

In 2001, Simon moved to Melbourne to work at The Diggers Club as a gardener. He was soon promoted to head gardener, a position he held for around eight years. It was here that he settled into his true calling: simple gardening. Not horticulture, not botany, but gardening.

'For the first time, it clicked in my mind that gardening is a different pursuit to botany and horticulture – it has an artistic element of blending colours, textures and shapes. It's a creative pursuit. People always say to me, "Oh, you're a horticulturist, are you?" I think they think the word "horticulture" sounds fancier than "gardener", it gives more cachet and credibility. But I always correct them and say, "No, actually I'm a gardener".'

Simon's home garden is testament to both his creativity and incredible gardening skills. Thankfully, it's only half an acre. 'If it was any bigger, I'd end up killing myself – I garden very intensively.' I've never seen such artful, dynamic and cohesive planting. Every single plant selection and placement has been considered. It's the work of a true master.

'I find the element of husbandry really important in the garden. Being able to predict what a plant is going to do next and guiding it gently in the right direction so it can give its best is something I really enjoy. In music you have to perfect your technique first in order to express what you want. It's the same in gardening – you have to have really good technique in order to express what you want through your garden.'

Beauty, in Simon's garden, is both a strong presence and a driving force. He talks of the occasional glimpse of the eternal, offered when the elements contrive to create a fleeting moment of such beauty that his heart cracks open. 'It takes you to another plane, it makes your heart soar and you're granted a brief glimpse of something bigger and greater. You can't repeat it, ever.' It's beauty that keeps him coming back for more.

Whether playing music, or playing with plants, it's clear Simon is driven by a combination of creativity and mastery. 'To me, gardening is a new art form – I'm creating and exploring new things. Whereas with my music, I'm reconstructing old music on old reconstructed instruments. In a way, both pursuits allow the two different sides of my creative spirit to come through. One is about perfecting or reinterpreting something from the past and the other is about forging a way into the future.'

SIMON RICKARD ON CARE, CHANGE AND HUMILITY IN THE GARDEN

On gardening

Gardening is the most obvious thing in the world. If you look at cultures all over the planet, people have always gardened – often primarily for food, because ornamental gardening has long been the preserve of the rich and educated. The human urge to garden is strong. You see it everywhere. You see it with people who don't have any outdoor space growing house plants. Gardening is a fundamental part of being human.

Around ninety-five per cent of the time, gardening is hard slog, frustration, and unmet expectations, but five per cent of the time you're given a glimpse of the eternal. This is what keeps me coming back for more.

On care and technique

Music and gardening are both open-ended processes. It doesn't matter what level you start at, there are an infinite number of levels to aspire to. With gardening, because you're also interacting with local conditions like soil, climate and seasonal variation, you have to be quite agile. It's different to other technical exercises – it's not binary. There's no right or wrong.

On perfectionism

I definitely grew up as a perfectionist. The older I get, the more I'm learning to dial it back a bit. Perfectionism, while it sounds good on paper, is ultimately a recipe for anxiety. I try to aim for perfection, but I am getting better at not being too hard on myself when I don't achieve it. Gardening, in particular, has taught me humility. I try really hard to make my designs and my husbandry perfect, but I just have to let go and know that I've done my best.

On gardening and change

I hope that, through my work in garden design and communication, I can touch people's lives. That, in some way, I can get them thinking. There's a place for foot-stamping and there's a place for change here in the garden. You can change things in your own day-to-day life to improve your own and other people's existence. I see gardening as improving societies as well. The Victorians thought that gardens were morally improving. That's why they planted all the public parks and gardens that we now benefit from.

Challenging gardens

I like gardens that interact with me and challenge my preconceptions. It's like a good human relationship. Your best friends should both nurture you and challenge you. This is what my garden does. It keeps me honest.

HOME

TRUTHS

Changing the world, one

THOMAS WOLTZ

THOMAS WOLTZ SAYS HE'S NOT A VISIONARY BUT HIS OUTPUT
CONTRADICTS HIM. HIS LANDSCAPE ARCHITECTURE FIRM
HAS HELPED TO TRANSFORM TENS OF THOUSANDS OF ACRES
OF DEGRADED AGRICULTURAL LAND INTO RICH ECOLOGICAL
COMMUNITIES THAT PULSE WITH LIFE. HE GARDENS THESE
PLACES, NOT WITH A SHOVEL AND FORK BUT WITH HIS PENCIL
AND HIS MIND. HE CARES FOR THE EARTH AS ONLY A TRUE
GARDENER COULD.

COLOUR REFERENCE: TĪ KŌUKA (*Cordyline australis*)   LOCATION: GISBORNE, NEW ZEALAND

Farm at a time

'I cannot see cultivation of the earth and cultivation of the spirit as separate at all. The idea of stewardship and care over land is one of the most important portals to happiness. What I want to do with our work is to care with intent.'

Thomas Woltz is a landscape architect, architect and principal of Nelson Byrd Woltz Landscape Architects (NBW). NBW has designed hundreds of parks, farms, residential gardens and public memorials and has a list of awards a few kilometres long. We are meeting at Orongo Station, a vast 3000-acre property on New Zealand's rugged east coast. Thomas and his team have carefully stewarded this landscape for the last seventeen years, transforming it into an internationally regarded example of innovative conservation agriculture. The complexity of the project is reflected in the scale of the on-the-ground team, which includes farm manager, Kim Dodgshun, and conservation biologist and ornithologist, Steve Sawyer.

We arrive on a Saturday morning and immediately head off for a tour – six of us squeezed into a farm buggy, weaving our way from one side of the property to the next. Thomas is our driver and tour leader, zipping with great energy and enthusiasm from hill to hill, gate to gate.

The scale of the project is stunning. I've never before seen a designed landscape of such size and contextual, artistic and environmental consideration. Agriculture, conservation and cultural history are interwoven to create a landscape that speaks of the site and its stories, using design as a framework. It's beautiful, productive, restorative and reverential.

The ethos of care is inherent in NBW's process. 'We aspire to approach land with grace and dignity. We start by listening,' Thomas says. 'Part of listening is having scientists come and tell us what they see or what they know; having historians or archaeologists tell us what they see and what they know.' Each time NBW begins a new conservation agriculture project, they engage a local ecologist and spend a week on site with both designers and ecologists doing biodiversity surveys. 'We quantify reptiles, amphibians, birds, bats, all living creatures, including plants, on the site and then work backwards.' In the case of Orongo Station, their discussions with Steve Sawyer have lasted for years, not weeks.

Armed with this information, design is then used as a framework to respect and support local ecologies, address human needs and desires, communicate the stories of the land and foster beauty. Care is taken to consider each of these outcomes equally.

'This is one of the most exciting places to bring somebody,' Thomas says as we stand on the side of a hill looking out over a citrus orchard. 'The composition is painterly, like a Frederic Church or Capability Brown landscape, but unlike those artists whose primary goal was aesthetic beauty, our aesthetic beauty grows from the geometry of a productive landscape married with the ecological landscape. The interweaving of those two things is a really important balance to strike.'

It's a view that clearly illustrates Thomas and his team's thoughtful and layered approach to landscape. The citrus orchard has been designed in service to production – addressing practical considerations such as turning circles, planting distances and wind protection – but it's laid out like an artistic composition. The river winding through the landscape has been fenced off and planted with native vegetation as a safe haven for native fauna, the road through the orchards has been designed to focus awareness on the historic Ngai Tāmanuhiri cemetery mounds in the distance and a previously degraded wetland has been revegetated. It's an example of the power of design in creating a framework for land stewardship, production and beauty.

'I think the future of conservation really lies in discovering these hybrid ecologies with agriculture. We're going to have to keep farming, but in ways that have much less of an irreversible footprint on land. I think it's really important work to be doing.'

We look out over another masterpiece – a vast seventy-five-acre reconstructed wetland that serves a number of important ecological functions as well as being a bold, graphic, living artwork.

The area had originally been wetlands but previous owners had drained it for cattle grazing. 'We invited water back into this landscape, but in a way that will read as a composition, as a giant painting.' The needs of birds were the driving force of the project. Each of the islands has been designed in consultation with Steve Sawyer to ensure they are the right size and topography for the threatened local bird species. Ribbons of revegetation lead up from the water's edge to the tops of surrounding hills so the birds can forage safely.

On the property's northern tip, the NBW team, in consultation with conservation biologists, horticulturalists and Māori officials, have installed a 2.4-metre fence around an eighty-six-acre area and planted over 50,000 trees to provide a refuge for communities of native birds, reptiles and invertebrates. 'These headlands are a very important wayfinding device for migratory birds. The team has created an incredible habitat for them.'

The seabirds, particularly the petrels and shearwaters, have a symbiotic relationship with the tuatara, the last survivor of an order of reptiles that thrived during the age of the dinosaurs and are extinct on the New Zealand mainland. The tuatara lays its eggs in the birds' burrows. In 2012, sixty-five tuataras were introduced into the enclosure, with approval from Māori officials. We spot some of the little reptiles as we walk towards the headland. They're incredible creatures, like mini-dinosaurs. It's the first time Thomas has seen them in the enclosure. For the first time in our visit he's lost for words.

We continue to wind our way around the cliff face as the sun sinks into the ocean, until we reach a limestone headland awash in birds. We sit quietly and watch as gannets, fluttering shearwaters and grey-faced petrels fly in to roost. 'These birds have returned to this headland for the first time in a century. And they're safe and they're reproducing,' Thomas says, with obvious emotion.

It's dark by the time we make our way back to the farmhouse. A sense of humility and awe envelopes us as we tramp through the bush. The six of us are connected to the vastness of the landscape in different ways and by different threads, but we share a sense of reverence and care. Love, too.

'I feel like the luckiest kid on the planet. Everyone asks me why I work so hard, but I don't think of it that way,' Thomas says. 'I am suddenly very conscious of my own expiration date. Not in a morbid way, but in a motivating way. If I have access to doing projects like this, I want to get them done, or at least started. Because this goes way beyond me or the property owner or my firm. It's really an ethos about how to address land.'

Thomas's ethos is grounded in care. When we think about ways of actively caring, it's often on a small scale. We talk about caring for a person, a garden or a pet. It's easy to nurture what is close to us. It's much harder to care for ideas and existences external to our own. What is astounding about Thomas is the expansiveness of his attention. Nothing escapes his care, from the detail of plantings in a garden bed, to design as a way of encouraging a paradigm shift in the way we relate to landscape, to ironing his employee's shirts as we talk.

Here's a truth: Love underpins care. When you love something or someone, you do everything in your power to care, protect and heal.

Thomas Woltz is a man in love with the world. Somehow, I feel this explains everything.

CHANGING THE WORLD, ONE FARM AT A TIME

HOME TRUTHS

THOMAS WOLTZ ON STEWARDSHIP AND STORY, CHAOS AND CARE

On vision

I want to make visible the ecological and cultural histories of land, but in a lens appropriate to our generation. I'm not just interested in stories of inequity or isolation or damage or destruction, I'm also interested in the beautiful, incredible stories of discovery through plants, including food, fibre and medicine. If we see the land – including the plants – as the repository of those stories, then the land is full. Our Western view of the land as empty until improved is a giant obstacle to the kind of stewardship that we aspire to.

On landscape as story

Landscape architecture is often reduced to an image of a pretty garden. I don't mind making a pretty garden but there's got to be a serious story underpinning the design. Somebody might come to a big, public park and have a great day throwing a frisbee, having a picnic and then go home. But if they scratch the surface and start to ask questions or look into how it was designed, how it all holds together, that's the story. This is what starts to build the emotional relationship between people and place.

On gardening

I absolutely consider myself a gardener. My tools in the garden are design and communication – creating a narrative and presenting it. We use design and narrative to protect fragile places and fragile stories. The design is what makes them visible, but that visibility then becomes the long-term protection.

On order and anarchy

I love nothing more than to create a frame for disorder, where nature is allowed to thrive and thrust and move and wriggle around within that structure. A design might begin as one thing, which then erodes and evolves into something else – maybe something much more beautiful than you ever imagined at the start.

On the vocation of care

The greatest happiness does not come from wealth or relaxation – the greatest happiness comes from an engaged life. All the wealth in the world can't buy care.

On hope

I'm very hopeful because I have the sense that the work my colleagues and I are doing together has the potential to set in motion large systems, both visible and invisible, that help creatures, including humans, orient themselves and feel connected in a dramatically changing world. We spend every day making places that will live beyond us and tell a story of the love of land into the future.

CHANGING THE WORLD, ONE FARM AT A TIME

From lawyer to garden

LESLIE BENNETT

THE SOIL HEALED LESLIE BENNETT. A DECADE AGO, SHE WAS AN
UNHAPPY LAWYER IN LONDON, WRITING PAPERS FOR THE US
DEPARTMENT OF AGRICULTURE ON FARMING PRACTICES. NOW SHE
SPENDS HER DAYS DESIGNING AND TENDING TO GARDENS THAT
ARE BOTH PRODUCTIVE AND BEAUTIFUL.

COLOUR REFERENCE: POT MARIGOLD (*Calendula officinalis*)   LOCATION: HILLSBOROUGH, USA

HOME TRUTHS

One day, Leslie Bennett had a conversation that changed the course of her life. 'I was sitting at my desk in London and an English farmer asked me if I had ever visited a farm. I told her I hadn't. "You should probably visit one before you keep writing about them," she said, not mincing her words.'

At that moment, the soil called to her from deep within. 'It felt imperative. It was like, "You've got to get to the land, now". I needed to figure out what my relationship to it was.' Leslie started visiting farms on weekends and loved it. This wasn't enough for her and she soon decided to quit her job at the law firm – 'which I hated' – and went to her father's birthplace, Jamaica, to work on a farm. 'It was such a healing path. I was clinically depressed as a lawyer and then as a farmer/gardener, I found myself. It's totally legit!'

Following her 'hard-core farming moment' in Jamaica, Leslie moved to northern California and began working on community-supported agriculture farms and gardens. She realised she was interested in more than just producing food, she wanted to create beauty too. 'I feel strongly that beauty and utility should be one together. They're not at odds with each other. When I was working on farms, the organic food movement often felt focused only on food, no frivolity. Then there's the pretty garden situation, where there's no room for production. Why can't we put our land to use to feed ourselves and our spirits, and at the same time be visually inspiring? Why would you not do that? I don't get it.'

With these questions in mind, Leslie began her own business. Pine House Edible Gardens is a landscape design firm that focuses on creating edible and beautiful gardens. It's a far cry from sitting at a desk in a law firm, and Leslie couldn't be happier. As we wander around a garden she created for clients in Hillsborough, just south of San Francisco, the smile doesn't leave her face. 'I really love what I do. I love creating beautiful places that have layers of meaning to them. What that meaning is, for me, is evolving. I really enjoy the intellectual side of things and there's a lot of space in the world of garden design to explore this.'

Leslie was engaged to design this garden six years ago. Her brief was to transform the space from a redundant tennis court into a highly productive, organic, edible garden that would nourish her clients and their autistic daughter.

'Food is medicine,' says the owner, Elizabeth Horn. 'With autism we take this statement very literally. We try to get kids to eat a clean diet and the best way to do this is to grow food yourself. That's why I contacted Leslie. We wanted to not only grow vegetables and herbs, but also create a sensory garden that would support our daughter's alternative treatments. It's made a huge difference to our daughter. But it's also impacted on our whole family. We are eating so much better now. We harvest everything out of the garden. The garden is such a healthy place to be.'

True to Leslie's focus on nurturing beauty and productivity, this is a fairytale vegetable garden. A series of raised timber beds house an incredible array of edible and insect-attracting plants. Peas wind their way up rusted metal arches and nasturtiums tumble exuberantly over the sides of the beds. Silverbeet, sorrel, eggplants, peppers and salad leaves are interspersed with chamomile, oregano, tarragon and more. It's a happy, healthy and nourishing space.

The other side of the garden is wilder. Here, a collection of stone-fruit trees are underplanted with a loose mix of larger edibles like artichoke (*Cynara scolymus*) and rosemary (*Rosmarinus officinalis*), insect attractors like poppies (*Papaver* spp.) and foxgloves (*Digitalis* spp.), and ornamental grasses. It's immersive and romantic and dispels the commonly held belief that productive gardens and ornamental gardens are two different things. They're certainly one and the same here.

The secret to this garden's ongoing beauty and productivity is the sustained care of Leslie and her team. Not only did Leslie design and install the garden, she also maintains it. Design is just the beginning of a garden's evolution; ongoing stewardship is by far the most important element. 'I learn so much with every garden. I think I love the maintenance more than the design. I just love being in the garden and seeing it change throughout the seasons.'

Being actively involved in the care of her clients' gardens was a conscious decision. 'I wanted to be really intentional with the business. I wanted to actually be in the gardens, talk to my clients and pick flowers – do the stuff I signed up to gardening for.'

Beauty and care. Leslie's work embodies the relationship between these two words. 'Creating beautiful garden spaces and somehow getting people closer to them helps people to care, to connect.'

Creating spaces that help people come home to themselves and the earth is a really important job. Yet, transitioning from law to gardening would not be described by many people as a stellar career trajectory. 'It's amazing to me how working with plants is so looked down upon. There are a whole lot of race and class issues wound up in this too, but, simply put, working with plants is not something that our culture encourages us to aspire to.'

In *The One-Straw Revolution*, Masanobu Fukuoka writes, 'The ultimate goal of farming is not the growing of crops, but the cultivation and perfection of human beings'. Many others, across many years, disciplines and backgrounds, echo his sentiment. If he's right, then the gardener, the grower, the steward of the land holds a role very much worth aspiring to. Leslie Bennett already knows this.

FROM LAWYER TO GARDENER

LESLIE BENNETT ON RACE AND GARDENING

On race and gardening

The two things that matter to me most are gardening and race. For a long time, I questioned how I could bring them together. They felt so disparate. I was like, 'This is gardening, it's so cute and pretty. These are racial issues, they're so challenging. What am I going to do?' It made me uncomfortable for a long time, but I've realised I just have to bring them together and talk about them.

My mother is English and my father is Jamaican. I grew up in a very liberal white bubble, where most people probably said they didn't see race. When I grew up and left home, I was racially and sexually harassed at work. It was then I realised that, as a black woman, racism happens to me. It wasn't my problem, it was theirs, but it hurt me, it really hurt me. It was so healing for me to begin working with plants and be out in nature.

For me, gardening has always felt like a really whitewashed space. When I was working on organic farms, I was always the only person of colour. Why is that? We all come from people who grew food, it's in all of our blood, and we all should have a relationship with plants.

In the last three years, I've become comfortable with what it means for me to be a black woman in the world of gardening. A lot of it is about being unapologetically black. I'm generally the kind of black woman that most white people can deal with pretty well – I have light skin, I'm educated, I grew up in the suburbs, I'm pretty palatable. I'm aware of that. I'm also aware that this is not the case for all black people.

I've started to shape my work so that I can more explicitly serve black women and the black community. Black women in America are bearing an extremely heavy burden. We, of all people, need a peaceful place to retreat to, a place of healing, a garden. I decided I needed to create gardens for black women.

I was recently awarded a small artist grant, enough to create my first black women's sanctuary garden in West Oakland. It's taken years of learning to be a gardener and a garden designer, while also learning to be a self-realised black woman. It's still a journey and it's not complete, but this is my first 'I'm going to do this. I'm going to bring it together and see what it looks like' moment. It's really exciting.

My next project is our home garden. I'm designing a garden for my son that reflects his cultural heritage. It's going to have a lot of Jamaican and English plants – lemongrass and tropical guavas, rhubarb and quince.

Raising a black boy in America is not a small undertaking. As a parent, I think it's important to give my son a compelling story about who he is, where he's from and what he can be proud of. I'm going to use the garden to do that. That's the story our garden will tell.

The insect lodge

MICHAEL SHEPHERD

A TANGLE OF WASHED OUT GREEN PRESSES UP AGAINST THE BLACK
TIMBER CLADDING OF THE HOUSE. FINE ARMS OF FOLIAGE LURCH
LEFT AND RIGHT, UP AND DOWN, THIS WAY AND THAT. THERE ARE
NO PATHWAYS OR PAVING. JUST PLANTS AND BUGS AND IDEAS,
AND MORE PLANTS. THIS IS THE GARDEN MICHAEL SHEPHERD
MADE A DECADE AGO – A GARDEN THAT PROVOKES MANY MORE
QUESTIONS THAN IT PROVIDES ANSWERS.

COLOUR REFERENCE: NEW ZEALAND FLAX (*Phormium tenax*)   LOCATION: ONEHUNGA, NEW ZEALAND

Who is a garden for? What can a garden be? Can a garden connect a site's present and past stories while contributing to creating its future? These questions roll around my head as artist Michael Shepherd and I ramble around his former garden, located on a quiet street in Auckland. Michael is a highly regarded painter whose work is found in international collections, and who has received the New Zealand Order of Merit for contribution to the arts. He is also a passionate gardener.

The garden took Michael 'many, many years of thinking and research' to create. 'I didn't want just another shit garden consisting of hedges and roses – the stuff that bedevils New Zealand.' He wanted to create a 'resolutely New Zealand garden' surrounding his home on a small suburban block.

We elbow our way through the front garden, weaving around a series of insect hotels and picking a pathway through tall shrubs and trees, being careful not to step on small understorey plants. Michael tells me the names and stories of each plant in the space. His knowledge is vast – he knows each plant's Latin name, where it originated, its relationship to the animals and insects it evolved with, and its cultural connections.

He points out rangiora (*Brachyglottis repanda*) – 'It's also called bushman's toilet paper'. Its leaves are like velvet. Then there's *Coprosma areolata* – 'Coprosma is endemic to New Zealand and was named by Joseph Banks. The root meaning of the word is "shit", from the Greek word *copros*. Banks named another New Zealand species *Coprosma foetida* – "smelly shit". It stinks!' Other plants he points out are bird, moth or invertebrate attractors. He knows about the earth too. 'I've always researched wherever I've lived. This site is of archaeological significance. The soils are Māori-made – they're extremely rich.'

I ask about his approach to making the garden. 'I started from the ground. What does the ground tell me? What is the archaeology of it? What can I do to keep that history intact?' After asking himself these questions, Michael decided on an ambitious project – an insect and rare plant conservation garden – as a way of listening to the site. And because 'I've always been a bit crazy about New Zealand insects'.

'I wanted to see if I could create a garden that could have ecological significance,' he says as we examine the leaf litter around the base of a tall insect hotel in the front yard. The hotel consists of a timber frame stacked with dried sticks. It provides plenty of space for small critters to create homes and stay safe from hungry mouths of predators. Pohuehue, or bindweed (*Muehlenbeckia complexa*), a fine, wiry climber with tiny round leaves and dark brown-red stems, weaves its way around the structure's base. It's considered by some to be a bit of weed, although it provides food for some of New Zealand's coastal butterfly species.

'I think the Western mentality has pushed all life to the edge, so what I tried to do in this garden was give the life on the edge a space to be. I wasn't going to knock anything out, I just don't believe in it.' Michael wanted the garden to 'push up against the house', to force visitors to interact with it. 'I wanted to create a garden that almost frightened people. In many gardens, the plant becomes an accessory and it's only there to decorate a human's life. When this garden was mine, I made people push up against plants, I made them struggle. I think those are good experiences.'

It's not just the physicality of Michael's garden that is challenging, it's the ideas behind it. 'I think the world can largely do without garden designers. Many of the so-called modernist gardens are completely inert. They're so huffed and puffed up and sprayed and looked after – all life is forced into straight lines. This is really problematic. We have huge amounts of these places in New Zealand. Mindless houses and mindless gardens. The garden should be an immersive experience; it should be ecological.'

Michael believes his experiment of creating an insect garden has failed. 'I knew the chance of failure was high, and in fact I have failed. Part of the reason is that the humidity is too high here, and the garden is too small. Nevertheless, I did get big influxes of all sorts of things that were lovely – lots of moths and birds. I had as many as thirty wax-eye birds (*Zosterops lateralis*) a day feeding here, until the cats moved in next door. I introduced the native cockroach (*Maoriblatta novaeseelandiae*). They lasted about three years until the rats cleaned them up. I couldn't get them to come back. Then I began reading theories about New Zealand bugs and I realised that once you disturb them, they won't return. You have to have viable forest for them to hide in and they'll creep out slowly if you plant the right things.'

From the insect hotels of the front yard, we meander down the side pathway, a shady area packed with plants that have been left to their own devices. Michael introduces each one, sharing its story and relationships. Kawakawa (*Piper excelsum*) is a plant with 'about a million different uses. It was used for compresses, it was used to ease pain, it was used as a kind of chewing gum to keep the mouth fresh on long voyages.'

Many of the plants are rare or threatened and (except the bottlebrush (*Callistemon citrinus*) in the front garden) all are endemic to New Zealand. They're all incredibly beautiful – their small leaves, varying forms and many shades of green foliage reward closer inspection. 'It's important to me to see the beauty in the ordinary. Many people suffer optical diabetes. They just want flowers.'

Michael's garden has everything except flowers. It's not a space to be viewed from afar, but up close, squatting down on the ground, seeing the light and shadows and bugs, touching the leaves and sticks and soil, and feeling the histories hidden beneath the earth.

Creating a garden that celebrates the potential of the garden as a sanctuary for all life forms is no failure. Creating a garden that rails against the monotony and ecological sterility of cut-and-paste modernist landscapes is no failure. Creating a garden that celebrates the stories contained within the earth it grows from is no failure. From where I stand – under the shade of a manuka tree (*Leptospermum scoparium*), in the shadow of Michael's deep passion for plants, place and bugs, and with a head full of questions – the garden can only be one thing: a great success.

Witches and weeds

MARYSIA MIERNOWSKA

MARYSIA MIERNOWSKA IS A GARDENER, HEALER AND SELF-DESCRIBED GREEN WITCH. SHE TEACHES MEDICAL HERBALISM AND PLANT CONNECTION AT THE GAIA SCHOOL OF HEALING IN CALIFORNIA AND BELIEVES MAKING COMPOST IS A SPIRITUAL ACT. PLANTS ARE HER 'GREATEST TEACHERS AND HEALERS'.

COLOUR REFERENCE: NASTURTIUM (*Tropaeolum majus*)   LOCATION: TOPANGA CANYON, USA

HOME TRUTHS

Marysia Miernowska puts on her black felt hat, wraps a woollen shawl around her shoulders and closes the front door. We head off, barefoot, for a walk in the hills behind her home in Topanga, a small community tucked into the Santa Monica Mountains, north-east of Los Angeles. 'My work is to help us remember that we are not just a part of nature, but we are Gaia herself,' she says as we wander down the narrow road, picking weeds and talking to trees.

Plants have been a constant presence in Marysia's life – from her childhood in Poland where her great-grandmother used to treat her arthritis by hitting her knees with stinging nettles (*Urtica dioica*), to permaculture and community gardening projects she worked on while studying architecture at university, to the mountain where she learned to communicate with them.

'I was living on the top of a mountain in Vermont, doing the whole "chop wood, carry water" thing. I was already talking to plants and hanging out in the woods a lot, so it was natural to get to know plants more, and learn how to make medicine. I undertook a medical herbalism apprenticeship with Sage Maurer of the Gaia School of Healing. It was a very spiritual journey. It took me to a place of wanting to be in devotion to the earth and to plants. I went really deeply into a practice of meditating with plants and communicating with plants and that's now what I teach.'

We head off the road and down a narrow dirt pathway flanked by bright green spring weeds. Marysia greets each new plant like an old friend. 'Weed' is not a dirty word to her. 'Weeds are the plants that matter. Mother Earth gives them to us in abundance. She's saying "Here you go, babies, stay nourished, stay grounded, stay wild and free"'.'

Marysia, as happy in the dirt as the weeds, glides along the pathway (the soles of her feet must be tougher than mine). She points to hills in the near distance where she often walks and talks with the plants. She loves the landscape here – she feels a calling to connect to it and nourish it. We stop and nibble on the bitter and spicy flowers of wild mustard (*Sinapis arvensis*), and discuss the plant's healing properties – 'the flowers help clear the sinuses and stimulate the digestive system' – before heading onwards, accompanied by a very happy, vagabond dog. He soon heads home. We continue on the pathway flanked by weeds, towards a tree dear to Marysia's heart.

Weeds are a big part of the tradition of herbalism Marysia practices – the Wise Woman tradition. 'It's folk medicine, the oldest form of healing.

In the scientific tradition of healing, death and disease are seen as the enemies, things you want to fight at all costs. Typically, the perfect cure is an odourless white pill and the power is put into test results and into the science ... The body is seen as a collection of parts – a heart, a circulatory system, a liver – it's not seen as connected or whole, or as greater than the sum of its parts. In the Wise Woman tradition, power is put into the hands of the person seeking healing and change. Death and disease aren't seen as the enemies or the result of toxins, they're seen as natural allies for transformation.'

Her preferred plant remedies are weeds and plants that are found in abundance. 'This is a tradition of healing that belongs to everyone, is accessible and is all about weaving relationships with the earth.'

Awakening people to their ability to learn from plants themselves is an important element of Marysia's teaching. This often starts with a plant meditation. 'We drink infusions of plants while dropping into a meditative state of listening.' Marysia then calls to the spirit of the plant to tell its story to the group. 'It's hard to explain the magic that occurs, but we learn how to both sense the medicinal properties of plants in our bodies, while opening our hearts to the spirits of the plants and listening to them with the wholeness of our being.'

When Marysia speaks of healing and being guided by plants, it's not just on a personal level. Her vision expands to the farthest reaches of the earth. 'The guidance of plants can help lead our consciousness back into the consciousness of the earth – so we can move and act and create transformation in a way that only humans can – from a place of deep listening to the earth.'

The garden is one of the places where our human connection to the earth is at its deepest, according to Marysia. 'If we are privileged enough to have a garden – and it really is a privilege – then we have an umbilical cord connected to the belly of Mother Earth.' Using the garden to nourish the earth is a powerful choice. 'We can change our environments by the way we garden. We can sequester carbon, increase water retention and boost soil fertility. We can also ask questions like, "How can we be medicine for the earth? How can we garden in a way that is regenerative?"'

We reach the tree Marysia wanted me to see. It's the grandmother oak *(Quercus agrifolia)*, named by Marysia and her daughter, Flora. They visit her often. We sit under its canopy. Marysia blends elegantly into the leaf litter. I recline too (somewhat less gracefully), so I can pick the spiky leaf tips of fallen oak leaves out of the soles of my feet. We talk about witches. Marysia is one and suggests I am too. 'One of the reasons I call myself a witch is to heal that word and to reclaim it. A witch is someone who lives with the cycles of nature and who uses and embodies them to create transformation and healing. The green witch is the one who speaks and listens to the plants.'

After our walk, we sit in the sun in Marysia's garden, drinking a special tea she has blended from nettles and other weeds. A swallowtail butterfly sips the nectar of sage flowers and nasturtiums run wild. Marysia speaks of the jasmine plant's desire to engulf the house. Small seedling trays of plants wait to be planted by Marysia's green fingers and a compost pile simmers in a shady corner.

For Marysia, the garden abounds with lessons and magic. 'In the fall, Gaia is starting to move into the current of death, decay and release. The plants' energy is going into their roots while their tops are going brown and dying off. This is when we cut things back in the garden. This is also a perfect time to be thinking about what we are releasing, what can we give death to in order to create more life in many moons to come. Even creating compost piles is a spiritual practice.'

I've met few people who are as humble in their relationship to plants as Marysia Miernowska. Her reverence for them runs deep, unrestricted by common assumptions of their value, or lack of. To her, they're everything. 'Plants have been my greatest teachers and healers. I'm just a little human being with limited amounts of experience and years on this planet, but from them I am learning from thousands of years of wisdom. The plants talk to me and tell me things. They give me spiritual and practical wisdom I could have never come to on my own.'

After walking barefoot in the hills, eating weeds and talking to the oak trees with Marysia Miernowska, I decide I'm happy to be a pastel green witch – I've got plenty of learning to do. Marysia, on the other hand, is a fluorescent green witch.

MARYSIA MIERNOWSKA
ON DEATH AND LOVE, SMOKE AND SOIL

On death

I think a lot about death and how important it is for us to cultivate a really embodied and intimate relationship with it. The garden teaches us this. The gardens that are bursting with life, that are the most fertile, are the ones that are completely rich in death and decay. Our society pushes for eternal summer, eternal growth, eternal beauty. Beauty, through this lens, means life. But death can be as beautiful as life. If we want to create something, we also have to take it apart and compost it. Death is what creates the next wave of creation. If we're just trying to create, create, create, without giving equal time to the dying process, we're not riding a regenerative current.

On soil

I make soil to create balance. We take so much from this generous planet. Soil sustains our civilisations. Her fertility allows the ecosystems that we rely on to thrive. I make soil, in gratitude for all I receive. And by making soil, I feed Her in return. And in this act of giving, I receive so much.

On love

Love is the greatest healer and the greatest force in the universe. If we can help people fall in love with the earth and fall in love with themselves and with spirit, then their genius is awakened as well. There is a great transformation waiting to be birthed. To do this, we need activated humans rooted and awake and in deep love.

On making weed infusions

Some of my favourite medicinal weeds to drink are nettles, dandelion root, raspberry leaf, chickweed and burdock root. All of these plants are rich in vitamins, minerals and enzymes. They bring us vitality, strengthening the body while gently cleansing the blood and organs, and they teach us to be like them – wild and free.

To make an infusion of dried or fresh roots or leaves, take a handful of the plant material and put it in a 950 ml jar. Top off the herbs with boiling water and cap the jar so the medicine does not evaporate with the steam. Let it infuse overnight. Strain, and drink some on an empty stomach first thing in the morning. Drink the rest throughout the day.

On burning herbs

Burning blessing herbs is a way to create sacred space, clear energy and shift consciousness, while making offerings to the Spirits. There are many aromatic herbs and resins that can be used as blessing herbs.

White sage is one of the best-known herbs for burning. It is native to Southern California but is over-harvested. I never harvest it from the wild and teach students to plant it instead. A Chumash medicine man taught me the important practice of burning only one leaf in prayer to cleanse a person or space, not an entire bundle.

If you have pine trees in the wild where you live, you can harvest your own resin by checking the base of the tree on the ground for any drops that have fallen. Never take resins from the tree itself – if it is on the tree, the tree is likely using the sap to cover a wound and heal itself. Comb your fingers through the soil below and you are bound to find some 'tears' of resin that you can burn into sacred smoke on a hot charcoal.

Art advocating for nat

JANET LAURENCE

JANET LAURENCE IS A HIGHLY REGARDED ARTIST WHOSE ART
PRACTICE DRAWS ATTENTION TO THE FRAGILITY, BEAUTY AND
IMPORTANCE OF THE NATURAL WORLD. HER HOME GARDEN IS
WHERE HER IDEAS OF NATURE AND CONNECTION ARE NURTURED
AND GROWN. JANET'S ART PRACTICE, CULTIVATED IN HER GARDEN,
CHALLENGES US TO RETHINK HOW WE SEE THE WORLD AND OUR
PLACE IN IT.

COLOUR REFERENCE: CREEPING FIG (*Ficus pumila*)   LOCATION: EAST BALMAIN, AUSTRALIA

Deep in thought and mid-conversation, Janet Laurence is unconsciously stroking a leathery gymea lily leaf. We're talking about art, plants and hope, as her dog, Muddy, tunnels his way through a clump of tall grasses. I have invited myself over following a conversation a few months earlier. 'My garden is a sort of renegade garden,' she told me. I was in.

It isn't just her garden I am interested in. I'd known of Janet's work for many years. When I was a small-town high-school student, I visited the Museum of Sydney and stood amid the murmurings of *Edge of the Trees,* a sculptural installation that she created in collaboration with Fiona Foley. I was deeply affected by it. Now I'm interested in finding out more about the role that plants have played in the evolution of Janet's art practice over the course of her career.

Janet's works are collected nationally and internationally, she's won a swag of awards, residencies and grants, and is regularly commissioned to create public artworks in Australia and overseas. She works from an inner-city studio and for the last fifteen years she has lived and gardened in a former gunpowder bunker.

'I've always been interested in nature, but before moving here I'd never had a garden. At my studio I have a lot of plants but they're more experimental. It's been amazing to have the opportunity to create a garden. Before, I'd always been confined. Gardening is a lot like painting to me. It's like I've made something that's almost part of myself in a funny way. I have to stop myself sometimes – I did some gardening this morning and I just went, "Oh my god, I've got to go to my studio and do some work!"'

If Janet's garden is a personal expression of her inner nature, her artwork exists on another plane entirely. She has become a spokesperson for those unable to speak: the trees, the coral dying in the Great Barrier Reef, and the plants she places on life support in galleries across the world. 'When I'm creating an artwork, I'm definitely wanting to wake up awareness in the public. I'm definitely wanting it to be a reflection on the wider world.'

Janet's work explores the aesthetics of care. She puts plants – uncommon in gallery spaces to begin with – front and centre. Often they're displayed in the highly humanised framework of a hospital, hooked up to intravenous drips with their branches wrapped in gauze.

Taking plants out of their usual context and placing them in a gallery, simply and elegantly highlights the plight of the non-human world in the face of humanity's ever-increasing demands for resources, space, food and water. 'By creating a situation that can be recognised as a place of care, like a hospital or sanatorium, people will become aware that these things must be cared for. It's an attempt to ask for, or incite, a need to care.'

Janet's voice, carried through her artworks, is strong, increasingly political and ultimately hopeful. It's a voice she's grown into over many years of creating art about nature and our environment. 'I think for a long time I was focused on gently waking people up, but now I feel it's imperative to speak loudly. I know that art can reach people. We need art now, we really need it.'

Art can touch hearts and make people listen in a way that facts and figures can't. 'Often the artist can speak when the scientist can't. They have to respond to the exact data, whereas the artist can play with it and present it poetically and emotionally. It's very, very, very important now for artists to be very active in their work.'

'Sometimes, I think it's too late, that people don't care anymore,' she says. 'It's like the world has turned into this place where it's only about money and nothing else. I cannot comprehend why so few people, just because they have money, are able to control everything, when we who want to care for the planet are so many.'

Janet justifies her work as a space to find hope. 'It's interesting how many people say to me, "Do you realise that most people don't care about anything?" I just can't believe that. I don't want to believe it and I won't believe it. You've always got to hope, because hope will enable you the space of possibility, and then you have the space to act. If you don't have that, what are you going to do?'

Janet's hope, vision and commitment to expression are embodied in the wild and exuberant garden that spills onto the nature strip in front of her house. Native ferns and mosses march up the entry stairs of her home and a creeping fig winds its way indoors through an open window. Her conversation with plants is collaborative, open and hopeful.

One of the great powers of art is to make us see: see the present and past in new ways, see reflections of ourselves and, perhaps most importantly, see our way to a better future. While our politicians continue their noisy and increasingly dangerous practice of pretending that it's business as usual, artists like Janet whisper songs of hope, drawing our attention to the interconnectedness, beauty and fragility of all life on planet Earth. Because, as Janet asks, 'What are we going to do otherwise?'

ART ADVOCATING FOR NATURE

The permaculture revo

DAVID HOLMGREN

IT IS NOT AN OVERSTATEMENT TO SAY THAT DAVID HOLMGREN HAS
CHANGED THE PLANET FOR THE BETTER. HE IS THE CO-ORIGINATOR
OF PERMACULTURE AND FOR THE PAST FORTY YEARS HE HAS LED
A REVOLUTION FOCUSED ON LIVING LIGHTER, BETTER AND MORE
IN TUNE WITH NATURE. HE IS, AS EXPECTED, A SELF-CONFESSED
'PLANT NUT'.

COLOUR REFERENCE: CHERRY TOMATO (*Solanum lycopersicum var. cerasiforme*)   LOCATION: HEPBURN, AUSTRALIA

ution

THE PERMACULTURE REVOLUTION

HOME TRUTHS

'The act of gardening is radical,' says David Holmgren. 'The garden is a space where one engages in a relationship with nature and the idea that we're separate from it – either above it or as destroyers of it – falls away.'

David and I are rambling around Melliodora, the one-hectare permaculture demonstration property he shares with his partner, Su Dennett. He prefaced our tour with the warning that, as our visit is at the end of the hottest and driest summer in thirty years, the land is not looking its best. Although the earth is certainly dry, there's no lack of abundance. Silverbeet is harvested for dinner, ripe red jewels hang from two-metre tomato plants, and an old fig tree drips with delicious fruit. Bees buzz, seedlings lurch towards the sun, and borage grows from cracks in rock walls. The landscape is pulsing with life.

David conceived the concept of permaculture with Bill Mollison in 1978. At its essence, permaculture is an ecologically based design system for sustainable human living. It's based around three core tenets: care of the earth, care of people and return of surplus. David describes it as 'consciously designed landscapes that mimic the patterns and relationships found in nature, while yielding an abundance of food, fibre and energy for provision of local needs'.

Since 1978, David and Bill's ideas have grown into a global movement that has touched millions of lives and provides an alternative framework for people to interact with each other and the earth. Thousands of projects have been implemented all over the world, from small city gardens to farms and large communities.

Melliodora has been David's permaculture testing ground for more than thirty years. 'In the early days of permaculture, I was often seen as the quiet, practical person, and Bill was the big thinker. Really, that was me wanting to put some personal truth behind the big ideas. I was only twenty-three when *Permaculture One* was published and while I didn't feel like a fraud, I did want to prove the theories myself. It was also about discipline. I had always been a conceptual thinker – you can float around in the clouds but the doing, and the dealing with mundane realities, brings you down out of hubris and overconfidence. It grounds you.'

The garden at Melliodora is designed from the house outwards. Intensive crops like seasonal vegetables envelop the home, growing just outside the kitchen door like a living supermarket. As we wander further away, the landscape changes. Tree crops replace vegetables, chickens scratch around under lucerne trees (*Cytisus proliferus*), and a glorious old pear tree (complete with tree house) makes itself known. It was the only tree on the entire property when David and Su first arrived in 1986. 'There were lots of rational reasons for buying the property, but the pear tree was the emotional one,' says David. The tree is more than a hundred years old. It was planted by a miner who lived just a few metres away – the remnants of his hut are still visible. Once it was surrounded by mining leases, then by blackberries, but it's now flanked by abundance. If only it could speak.

Melliodora is a closed-loop system. Rainwater is collected and stored for plant and animal nourishment; goats both supply milk and control weeds; chickens transform food waste into fertiliser and provide eggs; greywater is treated for re-use; excess food is stored, shared and preserved; and buildings and gardens are designed to work with the natural conditions, not against them. Nothing leaves the property except surplus produce. It's an approach that makes sense. 'Permaculture design projects often start with a personal and household audit,' says David. 'Where does everything we depend on come from? Where does it go when we're finished with it?' These questions apply to all aspects of human existence, from water and sewage to transport and food. Permaculture thinking can be applied to anything from backyard vegetable gardens to urban design projects, communities to corporate structures.

The garden is often where many permaculture projects start, which is why permaculture is often viewed as simply a form of organic gardening. This misconception has an upside: gardening is generally seen as a safe and simple pursuit. David suggests this might be one of the reasons the permaculture movement has lasted for forty years, despite the deeply challenging nature of its ideas and concepts to existing economic and political structures. 'What could be revolutionary about gardening?' he asks, with a chuckle. 'Being non-threatening is very important in engaging people at times of social conservatism.'

Although the ideas behind permaculture stretch far beyond community gardens and chicken coops, the brilliance of the movement is that they're also found right there in the veggie patch, the compost heap and the garden. They are accessible, individual choices with potentially revolutionary outcomes. 'Even the idea of "Let's grow food for ourselves in the suburbs" – as innocuous as it sounds – is threatening. You only need twenty per cent of people to never turn up at the major supermarkets for those corporations to question what the hell is going on.'

Rather than fight the system by rallying against what's wrong, David's brand of permaculture is more about taking revolutionary tools and ideas and placing them in the hands of individuals, to experiment with and learn from and do what they want with them. It's less about mass movements and more about smaller, decentralised changes.

'Permaculture is about treating yourself as a guinea pig and saying, "Let's see if permaculture principles can be applied at a personal and at a household level". If we do this, then we achieve one thing – we've followed our own ethical paths. If it works out successfully, we've also had a good time and we've been rewarded.'

This approach, argues David, is different to the activist idea of sacrifice for the cause. 'Let's reward ourselves. If we succeed and have a good time, other people will say, "I can do that. I don't need the permission of the government, the bankers or the technical whiz-kids, I can just do it".'

After forty years of talking about a revolution, David knows a thing or two about communication and human behaviour. As is often the case, revolutionary speak is all about framing. 'Asking "How do we do things that are beneficial for ourselves?" is a much easier way to connect to people than asking "How do we stop doing things that adversely affect other things?" If you achieve the same result, you achieve both.'

Behaviour is one of the simplest things in the world to change, because humans are so incredibly flexible,' David says. 'Yet, behaviour is often the hardest thing to change. A cat that's given lots of food just lies in the sun getting fatter and fatter and doesn't do anything, even though it probably knows it would have a much better life if it was out hunting. We naturally fall into that state.'

David Holmgren's brand of revolution works for me. It's quiet, personal, grounded in the earth and transformative. 'The important thing is to be leading a life that is contributing to building a better world and minimising harm – doing something that's ethical and achievable in a completely mad world. And at the same time, enjoying yourself in a basic way that doesn't require trashing the planet and exploiting other people.'

We return to the vegetable garden where David tells me of the pleasures he finds in eating what they grow at Melliodora. 'It's become a bit of an obsession.' He shows me his 'wild' gardening technique, which involves grabbing handfuls of dried seed heads and scattering them around the garden bed. David Holmgren, the green-thumbed revolutionary, is certainly at home in the garden.

He does, however, suggest that it's time to ramp things up a bit. 'The time is really ripe to boost the revolutionary side of permaculture. I think a lot of the public are ready for something a bit more radical.'

How about that? Revolution disguised as gardening is on the up-and-up. Tell your friends. Tell your neighbours. Just don't tell the bigwigs. Let's surprise them.

DAVID HOLMGREN'S PERMACULTURE PRINCIPLES

Observe and interact
Beauty is in the eye of the beholder.

Catch and store energy
Make hay while the sun shines.

Obtain a yield
You can't work on an empty stomach.

Apply self-regulation and accept feedback
The sins of the fathers are visited on
the children of the seventh generation.

Use and value renewable resources and services
Let nature take its course.

Produce no waste
A stitch in time saves nine.
Waste not, want not.

Design from patterns to details
Can't see the forest from the trees.

Integrate rather than segregate
Many hands make light work.

Use small and slow solutions
The bigger they are, the harder they fall.

Use and value diversity
Don't put all your eggs in one basket.

Use edges and value the marginal
Don't think you are on the right track
just because it's a well beaten path.

Creatively use and respond to change
Vision is not seeing things as they are,
but as they will be.

Reproduced with permission from *Permaculture: Principles and Pathways Beyond Sustainability*, David Holmgren, 2002, Melliodora Publishing

LIFE WITH

PLANTS

Bromeliads Vs Camell

SUE AND PETER MILES

PETER MILES BEGAN CONFISCATING GARDENING TOOLS FROM HIS MOTHER, SUE, WHEN SHE WAS IN HER EARLY EIGHTIES. IT STARTED WITH THE MATTOCK. SUE WAS COMPLAINING OF A SORE BACK AND WHEN PETER ASKED HER WHAT SHE'D BEEN DOING, SHE SAID SHE'D SPENT THE DAY DIGGING UP PRIVET ROOTS. THE MATTOCK WAS PUT ON THE BLACKLIST, AND MORE TOOLS SOON FOLLOWED.

COLOUR REFERENCE: BEGONIA (*Begonia* spp.)　　LOCATION: WAHROONGA, AUSTRALIA

Peter Miles is now the sole gardener of his parents' half-hectare garden in Sydney. His mother, Sue, now ninety-eight, observes his work from her chair on the veranda. The garden they've shared for decades looks like the love child of a camellia collector and a bromeliad fanatic. Which is exactly what it is.

I visit them on a December morning, taken aback by the long camellia-flanked driveway and lush green planting. An old cherry tree drips with bromeliads, rhipsalis and tillandsias, and hydrangeas nestle among vrieseas, begonias and other botanical wonders. It is mesmerising.

Sue, the camellia lover, is beautiful, frail and gracious. Her eyes are warm and her gardener's hands tell stories of flowers picked, shrubs pruned and holes dug. Peter, the bromeliad fanatic, has warned her about our visit. 'I've been making notes on why we did certain things but I left the notebook inside,' she says. 'Anyway, Peter will get it.'

Sue and her husband, Richard, bought the property in the early 1950s. They built the house, cleared the land and got stuck into the garden. 'We had all sorts of ideas – I wanted one of everything!' Sue says, laughing.

Sue gardened and gardened, planting trees, azaleas, hydrangeas and plenty of camellia cuttings given to her by friends from the NSW Camellia Research Society. In her excitement, she got the colours all mixed up along the driveway. 'They were reasonably successful, though.' Peter isn't particularly keen on camellias, Sue says. 'I love flowers to pick, but Peter likes flowers just to be in the garden. And then Peter discovered bromeliads. I wasn't sure about bromeliads. But he's won me over now.'

Peter says, 'When Mum came to pick me up from school, I'd often find her in the gutter, picking oxalis flowers for dyeing. She was quite a free spirit. She was really connected to nature. I think it was an escape for her. Any time we'd be in the garden or the bush, Mum's face would light up. Her love of nature made a very strong impression on me.' Peter spent his childhood rambling around the garden or building rock walls and birdwatching at their property in the Blue Mountains. After school, he studied fine arts at university but soon realised 'there were no jobs in art'. He began working as a gardener soon after.

In the early 1990s, Peter began helping Sue in the garden. It wasn't a conscious thing, but it evolved as Sue became less able. 'Around this time, he discovered bromeliads. 'I used to love perennials and cold-climate plants, but they just don't work in Sydney. I discovered bromeliads in the last drought and have been crazy about them ever since.'

Peter's passion for bromeliads soon began to infiltrate the conservative camellia garden. Slowly but surely, Sue's beloved cherry tree was decorated with a wild collection of epiphytic jungle plants, and strange tropical species were planted among the hydrangeas, clivias and azaleas.

Now the greenhouse is filled with tillandsias, hoyas and begonias, the roof of the potting shed is covered in boxes of bromeliads and the cherry tree is spectacular all year round, not just when it's in flower. 'People at the front gate would never realise what's in here,' Richard says.

'It's like living in a park,' Sue adds. 'Peter has planted a lot of stuff we wouldn't have planted, but we love it. He's much more daring than us. We were much more conservative.'

Peter admits, 'I made some dreadful mistakes in the garden. I think I broke Mum's heart a couple of times. Mum took it very well, but I probably needed to be a bit more consultative.'

Sue disagrees. 'We work in harmony.'

Fostering a connection to nature through a love of gardening is a gift, a serious and important treasure often passed down from a parent or grandparent to a child. Sue has shared this gift with Peter and he is now sharing it with his son, Theo. Nurturing the gift means nurturing the garden, nurturing the garden means nurturing each other, nurturing each other means nurturing the ground we stand upon. And on and on it goes. Passing it down.

'Peter, you've taken over with my blessing,' says Sue.

Lessons from the world

FRAN BODKIN

AUNTY FRAN BODKIN IS A D'HARAWAL WOMAN OF THE BIDIAGAL
CLAN, FROM THE SOUTHERN PARTS OF SYDNEY. 'AUNTY' IS A TITLE
THAT IS GIVEN TO ELDERS, WHO ARE RECOGNISED AS CUSTODIANS
OF INDIGENOUS KNOWLEDGE AND LORE AND HAVE PERMISSION TO
DISCLOSE KNOWLEDGE AND BELIEFS. FRAN HAS DEDICATED MUCH
OF HER LIFE TO SHARING STORIES ABOUT INDIGENOUS KNOWLEDGE
OF THE NATURAL ENVIRONMENT.

COLOUR REFERENCE: GEEBUNG (*Persoonia linearis*)　　LOCATION: MOUNT ANNAN, AUSTRALIA

s oldest living culture

Fran Bodkin has a twinkle in her eye. It's early morning and we're wandering through the Australian Botanic Garden at Mount Annan, just south of Sydney. She chuckles as we stop next to a native hibiscus, 'Oh, I love this one. Western people put hibiscus flowers in champagne on their wedding day, right? Well, we use it as a contraceptive. It stops men from doing it!'

Fran was born under a tree in central Sydney. 'Dad was taking Mum to hospital when the wheel came off the car and hit the tree and that's where I was born. Given my passion for plants, it must have been meant to be.'

A gifted storyteller and communicator, Fran has studied arts and science at university, written a plant reference book called *Encyclopaedia Botanica* and is an Elder on campus at the University of Western Sydney. She works with Indigenous children to encourage their curiosity about the environment and help them prepare for university. Fran is a tireless campaigner for the recognition of Indigenous knowledge and cultural heritage and the keeper of stories passed down to her through generations of D'harawal people.

Fran is also a member of the Stolen Generations. Between 1905 and 1967, Aboriginal and Torres Strait Islander children were forcibly removed from their families and communities as the result of government policies. Fran was first taken from her family when she was three, but she ran away from her foster home and found her way home to her parents soon after. 'Dad taught me to read and write by the time I was three, and he used to take me down to Central Station and make me memorise all of the train stations in New South Wales. He'd say, "Remember, if ever you get taken away or get lost, find a railway line. Once you find a railway line you'll find a station, then hop on the train back to Central and walk home." And so I did.'

Fran's father was a scientist and her mother was a gatherer and storyteller. Fran went to university to work out how to explain the many things her mother had taught her about the world around her, based on ancient stories and legends. 'At university they told me that science is about measurement, and that you can only understand through measurement and experimentation. But Aboriginal science is about observation and remembering. We don't do this kind of observation any more. Now it's all done through a microscope. We're looking at the small bits, and forgetting about the effect these small bits have on the whole environment.'

Fran is passionate about the relationship between plants, animals and the wider ecosystem. She explains how Gymea lilies (*Doryanthes excelsa*) signal the migration of whales from the Southern Ocean. 'We can't see the ocean out here, so we can't see whether the whales are arriving or not, but we know that when the gymea lily flower stalk reaches the top of the leaves, the whales are coming up from the south.'

Fran believes it's only when we start to understand these complex relationships that we will be able to truly understand the environment we're living in. 'I think my duty in life is to create pathways. I don't know what's at the end of those pathways but I do know they're pathways of curiosity. If I can make kids curious, that curiosity might stay with them until they reach a stage where they can satisfy it with study and learning.'

The stories that are passed down through generations of Indigenous Australians were used to frame their interaction and understanding of the environment. Some of these stories are now being studied, dated and quantified by Western science. One example is research by ecologist David Bowman, which showed that the seeds of a solitary clump of palm trees (*Livistona mariae*) in Central Australia were originally carried there by people about 30,000 years ago. Indigenous people already knew this. They've passed down the story of 'the gods from the north' bringing seeds to Palm Valley for tens of thousands of years.

Fran also tells stories about the rise and fall of sea levels. Again, these tales that have been passed down through generations of Indigenous Australians were verified when scientists found middens on continental shelves. 'They realised our stories are fair dinkum.'

For Fran, every plant has a story. We pass by a geebung (*Persoonia pinifolia*), a native plant that is notoriously hard to propagate. 'The seed has to be passed through the gut of a mammal. A long time back, a botanist saw the kids eating the geebung fruit and he thought he'd give it a go. He grabbed a handful of fruit, put in his mouth and chewed it. He couldn't talk for two days because it dries out the salivary glands. He couldn't understand how the Aboriginal children could possibly eat this terrible fruit. But they didn't chew it all up like he did. They ate the pulp, then swallowed the seed. When you go into the bush and see a whole lot of them growing in a clump, that's where the toilet was.' Soon after, I meet a scientist doing her PhD in *Persoonia* reproduction. I suggest she go and talk to Fran.

The stories keep coming. Round-leaf mint bush (*Prostanthera rotundifolia*) is 'really good at keeping mosquitoes away when you're out camping. Just put a little branch on the fire at night.' The stories are not just about plants. 'The little black ants start building a mound around their nest four days before rain. The highest side of the mound will tell you the direction the rain is coming from.' Fran is a goldmine of knowledge. The stories she tells are interlocking pieces of a puzzle that connect people, plants, environment and ways of seeing. 'Everything is linked.'

The Australian continent is home to one of the oldest cultures on earth. For more than 60,000 years Indigenous Australians have cared for this land. This alone should be enough to encourage respect for Indigenous ways of seeing and relating to the land, and a deeper exploration of the knowledge that they hold. 'I think we're too busy at the moment looking to the future than learning from the past. But we need to understand the past to know what is possible in the future.'

As Bill Gammage writes in *The Biggest Estate on Earth: How Aborigines Made Australia*: 'We have a continent to learn. If we are to survive, let alone feel at home, we must begin to understand our country. If we succeed, one day we might become Australian'. Aunty Fran Bodkin is a storyteller who is helping us learn our country.

The anatomy of garde

MICHAEL MCCOY

FEW PEOPLE ARE AS COMMITTED TO THE NITTY GRITTY OF
KNOWING AND UNDERSTANDING PLANTS AND GARDENS AS
DESIGNER AND PLANTSMAN MICHAEL MCCOY. HE'S LIKE A DOG
WITH A BONE – AS TENACIOUS AS A TERRIER BUT, THANKFULLY,
A LOT MORE ARTICULATE. HIS HOME GARDEN IS TESTAMENT
TO HIS PASSION FOR KNOWLEDGE – IT'S A VERY BEAUTIFUL
BOTANICAL LABORATORY.

COLOUR REFERENCE: SPURGE (*Euphorbia nicaeensis* 'Copton Ash')   LOCATION: WOODEND, AUSTRALIA

I've known about Michael McCoy for years. He was a shining light when I was a young designer and writer with a head full of questions. Through his writing, he expressed the things I was feeling but didn't yet know how to say. He explored big ideas about the relationship between people and plants through the making of gardens. Michael's commitment to curiosity gave me the confidence to embark on the path of enquiry that I am still wandering today.

I'm excited to finally meet Michael at his home on the outskirts of a small country town. It's early on a cold autumn morning. It's glorious, of course. And freezing.

The plants in Michael's garden speak of a long, hot summer. The colour palette is a faded mix of the light grey foliage of spurge (*Euphorbia nicaeensis* 'Copton Ash'), the straw-yellow of feather reed grass (*Calamagrostis* x *acutiflora* 'Karl Foerster') and the soft burgundy of stonecrop (*Sedum* 'Matrona'). I love it. I love the softness of tone, the dried seed heads, and the enthusiastic punctuation of an occasional bright purple autumn crocus (*Colchicum* spp.). Michael loves it too, but in an 'it needs a bit of work' kind of way. 'When I come home, I just can't wait to get outside and see what's going on in the garden. It's nowhere near as good as I want it to be but, golly, the pleasure it gives me. I just love it so much.'

After a quick tour of the garden, we retreat to the warm living room for tea and a chat. Michael had 'zero interest in plants as a kid'. His parents were not gardeners. 'They were one of the first generations who didn't have to grow their own food and, therefore, were perhaps the most celebratory and delighted about their separation and non-dependence on nature for food production.' Plants entered Michael's life in his late teens, through tragedy.

'My father died when I was seventeen. He was in intensive care for six weeks. During that time, Mum had taken some plant cuttings from my Aunty Edna. They were sitting in a glass on the window sill. These things grew roots, and I was completely baffled. I was fascinated that something could hold onto life long enough to establish the organs required for it to become a self-sustaining organism. The fact that you could break off a small bit of something and regrow it was probably very amplified in its power at that moment, for me.'

Armed with his new-found love of propagation, Michael went on to study science at university. 'I went crazy with it. I had pots all over the verandah. It got critical – I had all these plants and I needed to put them somewhere.

At that point, I became obsessed with the idea of putting plants together effectively. I needed to know how to make them look like something.'

Michael's curiosity has served him well. It has taken him from a botany degree to a gardening apprenticeship with the National Trust, a decade working in large private gardens, and a stint living and working with famed writer and gardener Christopher Lloyd at Great Dixter in England. He's written books, designed many gardens while tinkering tirelessly in his own, and, most recently, presented garden programs on television.

The question of how to put plants together is the foundation of his continuing interest in plants and gardens. He is driven by a deep curiosity and a desire to understand principles rather than knowing rules. It's not about knowledge for the sake of it, it's about pushing scientific and artistic boundaries.

'How can I get beyond the facts to the principles, so I know how far I can bend things? I am obsessed with the anatomy of gardens. I want to know what is going on. What is making it work or not? Why am I responding this way? How can I replicate this feeling? As a designer, if you can't say of an amazing space, "I think I understand what it was that made me feel this way", you're powerless. Only by understanding the principle can you confidently replicate it. Only by being literate in a language can you write a beautiful novel.'

Michael's own garden is a testing ground, a place where he can indulge his curiosity, explore principles and play. 'Most of what I want to do in my own garden isn't really about creativity, originality or current thinking as much as testing my skills as a craftsman with plants, and how well I can execute an already recognised design "standard" of spatial design, planting design or hard landscaping.'

His steppe garden – 'a misnomer that will remain until something better presents itself' – is a low, naturalistic planting with a curved gravel pathway running through the centre. It is loose and immersive. The repetition of plants guides the eye through the space and the washed-out colour palette is soft and calming.

It started as a trial for a design project he was working on and its anatomy is dissected on his blog, *The Gardenist*. 'I know for a fact that the location I've chosen would work better with plants in the 1–1.8 metre range. The annoying thing is I can't quite determine why this is, and therefore can't work out if there's a way I can change the surrounds to make my 25 cm carpet planting look or feel more comfortable than it does ... The trouble with low plantings is that you always feel like you're on them, and never in them. They can only work when surrounding features or plantings create the sense of in-ness.' Michael planted a border of Italian cypress (*Cupressus sempervirens* 'Glauca'), trimmed to head-height. It works brilliantly – the dark green foliage contrasts against the lighter tones of low planting, and their tall forms provide a visual frame for the garden.

From the steppe to the raised kitchen garden, from his artfully arranged firewood stack in the paddock to the billowing perennial borders surrounding the house, Michael's garden is not a showpiece. It feels real. It feels loved.

'"Green fingers" are a fact, and a mystery only to the unpractised,' wrote Russell Page in *The Education of a Gardener*. 'But green fingers are the extensions of a verdant heart. A good garden cannot be made by somebody who has not developed the capacity to know and love growing things.'

Michael McCoy has green fingers. Not only is he passionate about the big picture– the whys and hows of gardening – his head for detail and his desire to know absolutely everything about plants is astounding. We spend a lot of time discussing the difference between biannual and stressed-out annual plants – a conversation I didn't know I needed to have. 'No-one else cares, but I cannot rest until I fully understand bienniality in plants. I just have to work it out.'

Gardening is a humbling pursuit. Most gardeners, no matter how deeply they have dived into cultivating the earth, will tell you they don't know much. Maybe that's because there's no end to a garden's making. Perhaps it's because the cultivation of beauty from the earth cultivates a sense of awe and wonder that overshadows human pride and the illusion of knowing. Either way, it's a lifelong passion for many, Michael McCoy included. 'The youngest of my kids is now at the age I was when I got infected with this passion. I look at all three of them and think, "Please, please, let some consuming passion descend on them like it did on me". It may have kept me relatively poor, but it's kept me very, very happy indeed.'

Confessions of a plant

BRUCE DUNSTAN

BRUCE DUNSTAN IS A SERIOUSLY OBSESSIVE PLANT HUNTER.
HE HEADS OVERSEAS TWICE A YEAR TO DISCOVER NEW SPECIES
AND BRING BACK SEEDS. EVERY TIME, HE DISCOVERS ABOUT TEN
NEW PLANT SPECIES THAT HE SHARES WITH EXPERTS ALL OVER
THE WORLD TO SPREAD KNOWLEDGE ABOUT THE IMPORTANCE
OF PLANT DIVERSITY. HE'S NUTS, BUT IN THE BEST AND MOST
IMPORTANT WAY.

COLOUR REFERENCE: AIR PLANT (*Tillandsia schiediana*)   LOCATION: NUNDAH, AUSTRALIA

junkie

LIFE WITH PLANTS

Bruce Dunstan's garden is like nothing I've ever seen before. It's jam-packed with air plants (*Tillandsia*). They cover every surface: the pool fence, the railings of the verandah, the walls, posts and screens. I am astounded. I knew he was a serious plant man but I didn't realise just how far gone he really was. 'I'm more of a plant junkie than a plant hunter,' he says. I think he might be both.

The shadehouse in the rear corner of his suburban backyard is sandwiched between a palm-lined pool and the boundary fence. Air plants cover every surface, indoors and out. A few other plant species have been allowed in too, like an incredible *Anthurium wendlingeri*, a *Pitcairnia archeri* and some others that Bruce has found on his plant-hunting trips. But it's the air plants that steal the show.

I don't know where to look, so I ask Bruce why he collects them. 'I like them because they're so weird looking. The first one that really took my fancy was a *Tillandsia streptophylla* at the Brisbane Botanic Gardens. It was a grey bulb with curly silver leaves and a flower spike of pink paddles that stood nearly half a metre tall. It looked like it came from Mars.' In the late 1980s, Bruce's partner came home with a bunch of air plants that a co-worker was getting rid of. That was the start of Bruce's collection. He now has hundreds of different species.

Given that Bruce's garden is dripping, very literally, with air plants, I assume they're his abiding passion. I am wrong.

'My real love is *Heliconia*. If I see a heliconia I get tunnel vision. If I haven't seen it before, I'll climb over things to get to it. I've been doing that for thirty years. I hate to think what I've missed because I've been so fixated on them.'

Bruce moved on from heliconias to collecting air plants for very practical reasons. 'Heliconias need plenty of space and protection from strong winds. My garden is too small and exposed, being on the top of a hill. Heliconias are also very tropical in their growing requirements, so I'll never be able to grow all of them in south-east Queensland.' Bruce is a collector – he needs to have *all* the species of a particular plant, not just a few. Air plants, being so small, work with Bruce's physical space and obsession for collecting.

Bruce has been fixated on plants since he was an eighteen-year-old studying horticulture. 'I'd always had an interest in nature but knew nothing about plants. After twelve months it just clicked. I found my passion.' There's been no stopping him since then. He made his first overseas trip when he was twenty. He'd joined the International Heliconia Society and ended up on a plant-hunting trip to Ecuador.

Just for a minute, imagine a twenty-year-old man joining a plant society and spending his holidays going to heliconia conferences and on plant-hunting trips instead of drinking and partying. 'I was the youngest member of the board of the Heliconia Society International for a while,' Bruce says. Of course he was.

Bruce has two older brothers who don't share his love of plants. Nor do his friends. 'They're not plant people. I've taken a few friends on a plant hunting trip and they've been amazed but it's not something they'd do regularly. I'm just a crazy plant person.'

I ask about the specifics of these plant-hunting trips. 'We cruise around and look for things out the window, then we stop and explore. We call it "car-seat botanising",' he explains. Alternatively, he can spend up to seven hours each day 'rolling around in the mud with a machete and boots'. Ten days of plant hunting is about all he can handle, because 'after ten days in the forest you're all scratched and knocked around and getting a bit infected.'

Bruce and his hunting companions have traipsed around Colombia, Panama and Ecuador, exploring plant-diversity hotspots, having run-ins with jaguars, meeting locals (who are often bemused by their botanical pursuits) and being awed by plants. 'A guy told me about a new road in Ecuador that veers off towards the Colombian border. We visited it and it was amazing seeing all these things that I've seen in books but I hadn't seen before. At the same time, though, there's the sound of chainsaws, and piles of stacked timber.'

Bruce visited Sabah, Malaysia, for the first time in 1988. 'We went back in 1993 and, where we had previously seen forest, there was just acres and acres of timber stacked three storeys high. It's all palm oil now, there's no forest left. Seeing things like that spurs me on to get out there.'

Bruce's passion for plants doesn't end at his boundary fence and isn't driven purely by the thrill of the chase. There's a serious undercurrent to his plant-hunting exploits, which is driven by his desire to spread an awareness of the importance of plant diversity. He is a very knowledgeable, and very passionate citizen botanist.

'It's been estimated that human beings know scarcely five to ten per cent of the plant species present on Earth, and from them we derive ninety-five per cent of all our most important medicines,' writes plant scientist Stefano Mancuso in *Brilliant Green: The Surprising History and Science of Plant Intelligence*. 'Each year, thousands of species we know nothing about become extinct, and untold gifts to humanity are lost with them.' Every time Bruce visits Colombia, he discovers around ten new plant species. It's an incredible gift to the world.

When he finds a plant he thinks might be a new species, Bruce sends photos to international experts for clarification. 'They will give us the nod, or not. Sometimes we might find something that was described back in 1860 and this is the first time it's ever been photographed.' He also shares his discoveries online. 'I place a lot of images on websites, to expand the knowledge. Even just taking photos and sending them to experts helps them get a better handle on species range. And if we go to areas they haven't been, it gives them an idea of where they should be planning to do research.'

If Bruce finds a new species, it's up to the taxonomists to classify and name it. It can take around twenty years for a plant to be named. Bruce hasn't yet had the opportunity to name a new species, but he has named a plant variety after his wife, Elisa. 'It's called *Heliconia regalis elisa*. It's pink and fuzzy and really hairy.'

A Californian cutting ga

MAX GILL

MAX GILL IS A FLORAL DESIGNER AND GARDENER WITH A LOVE OF
CLEMATIS AND DIRT. HIS PASSION FOR CREATING LUSH FLORAL
ARRANGEMENTS BASED ON HIS OWN HOME-GROWN BLOOMS
HAS LED TO WIDE ACCLAIM. BUT HIS GARDEN IS NOT JUST A
STOREHOUSE OF MATERIALS FOR HIS WORK. IT'S ALSO WHERE
HE FINDS SOLACE, INSPIRATION AND NOURISHMENT.

COLOUR REFERENCE: NASTURTIUM (*Tropaeolum majus*)   LOCATION: BERKELEY, USA

We arrive at Max Gill's old timber home in Berkeley, California, early one spring morning. He hands me a mug of extra-strong homemade coffee and we explore his dew-laden 'work in progress' garden. 'About four years ago I totally gutted it. I figured it needed a little more structure, some more trees and shrubs. But then life happened and work happened...'

It's wild space, consisting of raised cutting gardens for Max's floristry work, fruit trees and abundant planting. Gravel pathways lead through the garden and flattened recycled cardboard boxes are used as mulch and weed suppressants, with cuttings from his garden and studio composted on top. Clematis and roses grow wherever they desire – twining their way up trellises and trees. Nasturtiums (*Tropaeolum majus*) run rampant.

Much of the garden consists of plants Max has bought for use in his floral arrangements. Once he's done with them as cut flowers, they make their way into the garden, where he continues to harvest them for his work. He shows me his 'walk of shame' – pots of heucheras, hellebores and others that fill the side passageway. They are in limbo – awaiting their second life in the garden. They'll make it into the soil soon.

Max has always loved gardening. 'I would make gardens in the apartments I rented and leave them behind as I moved on', but he arrived at flowers in a roundabout, serendipitous way. After completing an environmental science degree at university, he worked in bars, walked dogs and waited tables. He knew he wanted to do something creative but wasn't sure what. 'A friend of mine liked the flowers I got her for her birthday, and when she got married she asked if I'd do her flowers. I had no idea what I was doing and I horribly underbought. It was 4 am and I had heaps of arrangements left to do, so I had to cut flowers from my garden and under the nearby freeway. It was super fun, and so compelling.'

At the time, Max was working in a bar. 'I mentioned to a customer that I had the best time doing my friend's wedding and he said, "You've got to meet my florist friend, Ariella Chezar, she's amazing". I met Ariella and she said, "Come with me. You can do this too." That was fifteen years ago.' Through Ariella, Max ended up spending three years 'schlepping buckets' for the florists at the acclaimed Chez Panisse restaurant run by chef, author and food activist, Alice Waters, before taking over the job himself. Nowadays, he's incredibly busy making arrangements for homes and restaurants, creating floral installations for weddings, and styling flowers for editorial work. Max has clearly found his feet, but it all begins and ends in his garden.

'My relationship to flowers began in the garden. I have always found it so gratifying to watch things grow and to propagate plants from seed. I'm uncomfortable if there's no dirt under my nails. Even when my season is at its busiest, I make an effort to have contact with soil. Sometimes the best I can do is do a lap of the garden, and then I return to the house and sit in front of a computer for a while, but maintaining a relationship out here – even if it's just pulling some weeds out of the gravel in the driveway – is really vital and so grounding.'

Although using plants from his own garden in his arrangements began as a necessity, that technique has become entwined into Max's practice, just like a clematis vine. 'I try to use natural principles. Very often the plants in my arrangements look as if they're all responding to the same environmental conditions – like shade, sun, wind and geographic location. What I find most compelling in nature is when plants are struggling to find their place in the environment. As they fight to overcome the challenges of space and light, often surprising us with their juxtaposition, they create beauty through adaptation.'

Max's work studio is an old timber shed in his backyard. A wheelbarrow rests against a raw timber wall, next to stacks of plant pots and flower boxes. Ivy winds around the corner of the building and a long, stainless-steel bench runs down the centre of the space. Offcuts of foliage and flowers are scattered over the shiny surface as Max makes an arrangement inspired by his garden. 'Doing an arrangement with a plant that you've known intimately since it was a seed is really gratifying.' Long tendrils of nasturtium are transformed from nondescript overenthusiastic garden plants into expressions of nature's exquisite design sensibility. May bush (*Spiraea cantoniensis*) also receives the Max treatment – a few branches from the bush in his backyard turn into the perfect white-flowered backdrop to a few poppies and narcissus that he sourced from a local grower. All of a sudden, there's a garden in a vase.

Max is fiddling with the flowers. He's worried the arrangement is not full enough, that it won't photograph well. He needn't be concerned. Max's arrangement, like any garden, is not a flat picture. It's an experience. Light dances with shadow, space opens and closes and detailed inspection rewards the eye. 'Having a beautiful visual experience alters your body chemistry. It's very nourishing to pursue beauty creatively. Putting something together yourself, and getting it to a place where it's pleasing for your eye, is a very healing thing to do.'

Max's pathway through and beyond the garden has been one of restoration. 'I've struggled, as many creative people have, with depression and anxiety for much of my adult life.' The dirt is where he returns to for solace, inspiration and hope. 'The garden reminds me of what's important. It's so easy to get caught up in the day-to-day, but to have a physical reminder of what I find most grounding is so valuable. The garden is my gem, it's my church, it's my therapist.'

A CALIFORNIAN CUTTING GARDEN

The garden as family

CLARE JAMES

CLARE JAMES IS AN ARTIST, A PASSIONATE GARDENER AND
A BORN NURTURER WHO HAS CREATED A BEAUTIFUL AND DEEPLY
PERSONAL GARDEN. IN HER GARDEN, SHE EXPRESSES HER WAY
OF BEING, HER DESIRE TO CARE, HER EYE FOR BEAUTY AND HER
DEEP LOVE FOR ALL LIVING THINGS – THE TIGER SLUGS SHE FEEDS
AT NIGHT, HER DUCK GLORIA AND THE PLANTS SHE CONSTANTLY
MOVES UNTIL THEY ARE IN THE RIGHT SPOT. THEY'RE ALL FAMILY
TO CLARE. HER CONCEPT OF KIN KNOWS FEW BOUNDS.

COLOUR REFERENCE: STONECROP (*Sedum matrona 'Autumn Joy'*)   LOCATION: HEALESVILLE, AUSTRALIA

LIFE WITH PLANTS

Clare James gardens, lives and creates art with rawness, openness and passion. All gardens are a human expression, but Clare's, perched on the side of a hill looking out over a small country town, is so deeply intertwined with her being that it's impossible to understand her without it.

The story of Clare's garden is woven with the story of her family. Clare and her husband Mark Boulet were married in the backyard and their children, Lylah and Olive, were both born in this house. Clare's sister, also an artist, lives close by and their mother's house is just 300 metres away.

Gardening, like art, runs in Clare's blood. Her father is a botanist and she spent much of her childhood in the vegetable garden with him. 'Gardening is in my blood but it's also a passion of mine. Creating and tending a garden gives me a total immersion in nature, which helps me feel grounded, gives me a regular workout, fills my world with beauty, inspires my art practice, feeds my family, shelters my pets and makes me deeply happy.' She couldn't live without it.

By day, when she's not making art in her studio, Clare's making art in the garden: planting, cutting, pruning, transplanting and growing. 'It's like I have a huge canvas, a 1700-square-metre canvas I get to paint with plants. Creating a composition that works from every single angle is so much fun. I love watching the artwork change over time and creating a connection with every element in it.'

Her canvas is full – there's a huge vegetable patch, an orchard, a duck house, chook house, tree house, trampoline, art studio and more. Like most well-loved gardens, it has evolved over the years in relationship to those who inhabit it – and not just the human residents.

'Learning how to collaborate with everyone and everything in a garden is a constant dance that I love being part of,' says Clare. 'Not only do I consider the needs of each individual plant I put in the ground, I also take into consideration its plant neighbours (aesthetically and spatially), the way my children, husband and pets use the area, the condition of the soil, current climate, rainfall and hungry wildlife. From the moment a plant is in my care, I try to make it as comfortable as possible and work to create the perfect balance for it to thrive.'

The act of gardening can connect us to the big truths of existence like few other pursuits. Clare's garden, as an extension of her ideas about the world, reminds me of three simple, yet powerful, words: *everything is connected*. Plants, fungi, slugs, stars, humans, dogs and ducks. Everything relates to everything else. Ignoring this truth is dangerous. As poet and gardener Stanley Kunitz wrote in *The Wild Braid,* 'The universe is a continuous web. Touch it at any point and the whole web quivers.'

Clare's small part of the web of existence is a place of joy, wonderment and love. 'I'm fascinated by all living things. I'm constantly in awe of nature and the craziness of what lives right here in my own backyard. This place is where I find deep happiness. The spiders and centipedes, birds and frogs, soil microbes and crickets all silently shout at me to look at them. I never tire of this, and find I take this wonder into the wider world with me.'

Her garden is also a place of deep connection to natural cycles and seasons. 'Gardening in a climate with defined seasons reminds me that I too am part of the cycle of nature. When I feel a crazy rush of energy and can't stop creating, cooking, digging or weeding, it feels as though I'm a garden being woken up by the warm, spring sunshine. Every cell in my body is bursting with excitement.' At other times, she feels the way her plants look at the end of a long, hot, dry summer: worn out, exhausted and wilting.

'We too are part of nature, and those of us who garden for the love of it know just how connected we are to the seasons, the changing weather and the number of daylight hours. Just as a garden will have many moods, changes, highs and lows, so too can I.'

The garden is not just Clare's domain; it's a family affair. The children are keen vegetable gardeners and Mark is the chief preserver. 'I grow the food and Mark preserves it. He's good at finishing jobs and I'm better at multitasking, which gardening allows me to do. There's no end, which is what I need. Mark likes a job to be rounded up and finished.'

Clare and Mark have built a space without lots of money, but with an abundance of creativity, love, lateral thinking and thrift. 'The garden has been grown from cuttings, swapping and sharing. I sift through markets for small, interesting plants and then work out how to make them grow,' Clare says. She points to a clump of feather grass (*Miscanthus sinensis*) and tells me how she spotted it in a vase in a shop in Healesville. 'I went into the shop and said, "I don't want to buy anything, sorry, but what is that plant? I don't have it." The owner cut me a chunk from her plant out the back and I just love it. I can't wait to divide it up and have more, more, more.'

Clare's garden is full of stories and soul. It's the kind of space that can only be created by someone like Clare – a passionate plant woman with sharp eye for beauty and a desire to live honestly, in close dialogue with the earth beneath her feet and all the lives it sustains. She's a born nurturer and has created an incredibly generous and inviting place of growth for her huge family of humans, ducks, birds, dogs, chickens, slugs and plants. It was a treat to spend a day in her world. I could have stayed all week, chatting about poetry and ducks, avoiding the not-so-friendly attention of Dobby the rescued Quaker parrot, and discussing what to do with overproducing zucchini plants. We part reluctantly, with promises of seeds in the mail and poems on the wind.

CLARE JAMES ON STARTING A GARDEN

My advice for beginner gardeners is to treat the soil as a pet.
If you spend time and energy bringing the soil to life, most
plants will thrive. The soil needs to be fed with compost,
watered, nicely tucked in with mulch – lucerne hay is my
favourite – and regularly checked to make sure everything
is looking good and smelling sweet. This way, you'll become
familiar with the fascinating world living in the soil and be
able to tell the difference between 'dead' and live soil.

EPILOGUE

It's raining. I'm sitting in our boatshed, watching the drops fall onto the water outside the window. The possums in the roof are rustling and the neighbour's dog is chewing sticks at my feet, grinding dirt and wet dog scent into the rug. This room, with its cracked concrete floor leaning towards the water, ancient, half-rotted timber window that barely holds glass, and philodendron roots creeping in from the gap between the wall and floor, has heard every word in this book. Sentences have grown from this place.

Moving away from the city has realigned my existence with my values. I live with the wind, soil, trees and water. Not separate; not insulated. It sounds romantic, and to a point it is. My heart sings with gratitude for the beauty I'm surrounded by every day. It still feels like a dream.

With romance comes reality. We've had no bathroom for nearly a year, no walls or windows for months, and our floor has more holes in it than a monstera leaf. The garden I've been dreaming of for decades is a shabby collection of wallaby-chewed plants and weeds, and my vegetable plot is the most heavily fortified landscape this side of the Korean Peninsula. It's not pretty, but beauty is hiding among the leaf litter, if you look closely. I am in love with this land. What it is now, what it has always been and what it might one day become.

This book has grown alongside my garden. Every person in it has been there with me as I've planted spinach seeds, poked around in the compost or rambled through the bushland behind our house. I've tested ideas, absorbed perspectives and found inspiration through the shared process of gardening both these words and the land in my care. The process of digging among the truth, beauty and chaos of my garden, while digging among the truth, beauty and chaos of their stories, has been a gift and an honour.

Love and care are the common threads connecting the stories in this book. I write of them within the context of the garden because it's a place that cultivates the spirit like few others. It's a wellspring of the silent and enduring force of beauty. It's an illustration of the gritty and grand mystery of existence. It's just outside the back door. It's where I've always found myself anchored.

For years, when I've had trouble sleeping, I've walked in my mind down the long driveway from my childhood home on the farm, greeting the poplar trees, kurrajong and ironbarks at the front gate. I walk down the dirt road towards town until I fall asleep. Recently I've been conjuring the dirt track leading from our house on the river instead – through the garden and into the bushland beyond. It's not imprinted yet, but its faint lines on my heart are slowly making themselves clear.

FURTHER READING

The Biggest Estate on Earth: How Aborigines Made Australia,
Bill Gammage, 2011, Allen and Unwin

Required reading.

Braiding Sweetgrass: Indigenous Wisdom, Scientific Knowledge, and the Teachings of Plants, Robin Wall Kimmerer, 2013, Milkweed Editions

A collection of essays overflowing with reverence and love for the natural world. A reminder of the deep interconnectedness between all life on earth.

Brilliant Green: The Surprising History and Science of Plant Intelligence, Stefano Mancuso and Alessandra Viola, 2015, Island Press

A passionate argument for recognition of the intelligence and importance of the plant kingdom. This book will change the way you look at plants.

A Continuous Harmony: Essays Cultural and Agricultural, Wendell Berry, 2003, Shoemaker and Hoard (first published 1972)

Farmer, poet, writer and environmental activist Wendell Berry is a beacon of integrity, insight and inspiration. His words are always worth reading. And rereading. Repeat.

The Gardener's Year, Karel Čapek, 2002, Modern Library (first published 1929)

An entertaining and intelligent unpicking of a year in the garden from one of the Czech Republic's greatest authors. It's overflowing with wonder, humour and truth.

Gardening at the Dragon's Gate: At Work in the Wild and Cultivated World, Wendy Johnson, 2008, Bantam Books

An entertaining and insightful musing on life and spirit in the garden by a passionate Zen practitioner and gardener.

Gardens: An Essay on the Human Condition, Robert Pogue Harrison, 2008, University of Chicago Press

A thoughtful exploration of the relationship between gardening and the cultivation of the human spirit. An important book.

Landscape and Memory, Simon Schama, 1995, Random House

A big, dense book exploring the human connection to landscape, viewed through the myths and traditions of Western culture. I'm not done with it yet.

The Man Who Planted Trees, Jean Giono, 1996, Harvill Press (first published 1953)

A legendary allegorical tale of a shepherd who reforests a barren landscape, one acorn at a time.

New and Selected Poems: Volume Two, Mary Oliver, 2005, Beacon Press (first published 1992)

'Be ignited, or be gone.' You can't beat poet Mary Oliver for words on the wilderness inside and outside of us.

A Philosophy of Gardens, David E Cooper, 2006, Oxford University Press

A thoughtful and eloquent exploration of the importance of gardens and the act of gardening.

RetroSuburbia: The Downshifter's Guide to a Resilient Future, David Holmgren, 2017, Melliodora Publishing

A practical and philosophical permaculture manifesto for a changing world.

Source: Nature's Healing Role in Art and Writing, Janine Burke, 2009, Allen and Unwin

This book explores the important relationship between creativity and place. The connection between childhood Edens and creative output is something I hadn't considered deeply before reading this book.

Second Nature: A Gardener's Education, Michael Pollan, 1991, Grove Press

Reading this book confirmed my preliminary inklings that the garden is fertile ground for the contemplation of broader questions of humans and environment.

The Tree, John Fowles, 2010, Harper Collins (first published 1946)

A powerful meditation on the natural world and human creativity.

The Wild Braid: A Poet Reflects on a Century in the Garden, Stanley Kunitz with Genine Lentine, 2007, W.W. Norton & Company

Life, poetry and the garden through the eyes of one of America's most beloved poets. A soulful, thoughtful gem of a book.

ACKNOWLEDGEMENTS

There are scores of people who have contributed to this book, in ways large and small. The ideas at its foundation have grown from hundreds of conversations, ideas shared, and endless acts of generosity, kindness and trust over many years.

Our biggest gratitude goes to each of the people included in the book. Thank you for taking the time to meander with us for hours, and sometimes days. You indulged our many questions, resigned yourselves to trying to look natural as Daniel snapped pics, and submitted yourselves to our occasionally awkward and often dreadful jokes. It was an honour and joy meeting all of you. You are this book.

To our publisher, Kirsten Abbott – your trust and ever-so-diplomatic massaging of our vision and output has resulted in a book we're both incredibly proud of. Evi O, designer, friend, and owner of the naughtiest/cutest whippet in Marrickville – thank you for holding our hands through many iterations of this book. You've gone above and beyond to make it as special as we wanted it to be.

To the generous people who pulled strings, thank you. David Godshall, for being our Californian plant person fixer (we'd still be lost in the streets of east LA if not for you); Claire Takacs, for lining up dinner at Cevan Forristt's house (an experience we're unlikely to forget); Xanthe White, for pointing us in the right direction in Auckland (and sharing your birthday lunch with us); and Paul Appleton from Nelson Byrd Woltz, for helping us get to the wild east coast of New Zealand (and cooking dinner).

FROM GEORGINA

To Peter and Wendy Reid, my parents. Thank you is not enough. You have given me space to come home to myself. For this, and so much more, I am incredibly grateful.

To Ameli Tanchitsa. You are my earth. Thank you for grounding, nurturing and loving this wayward plant.

To *The Planthunter* website readers, contributors and friends. In particular, thank you to Lucy Munro for guiding *The Planthunter* ship while I've been holed up writing this book. Thank you to all the *Planthunter* contributors over the years for trusting me with your stories, visions and hearts. Last but certainly not least, thank you to *The Planthunter* readers for coming along for the ride – I had no idea anyone but my mum would want to!

FROM DANIEL

To Maureen Gregg. Thank you for being the most caring and generous mother I could wish for.

To Christophe Vivien. Thank you for bringing such perspective and joy to my life.

First published in Australia in 2018 by Thames & Hudson Australia Pty Ltd
© Georgina Reid (text) 2018
© Daniel Shipp (photography) 2018, except pp. 24 and 253 © Wendy Reid
All rights reserved.

North American edition published in 2019 by
Timber Press, Inc.
The Haseltine Building
133 S.W. Second Avenue, Suite 450
Portland, Oregon 97204-3527
timberpress.com

Design: Evi-O.Studio | Evi O.
Editing: Lorna Hendry
Printed and bound in China by C&C

ISBN: 978-1-60469-964-7

A catalog record for this book is available from the Library of Congress.

ABOUT GEORGINA AND DANIEL

Georgina Reid is a writer, landscape designer and the founder and editor of *The Planthunter*.

Daniel Shipp is an award-winning Sydney-based photographer. With a thirst for light and form, he crafts images into emotive narratives, telling stories about the worlds within this world.

GEORGINA ON DANIEL

Daniel is a phenomenal photographer and artist. His work is honest and raw and his images are never just pretty pictures, they're highly considered and richly woven stories of people and places. A keen observer and incredibly curious soul, Daniel always manages to get beneath the surface – to the heart of the matter.

Not only is Daniel a brilliant photographer and good pal, he's a walking electronics shop, chemist and (since working with me) food store. We've travelled a lot together for this book and, though I'd like to think he finds our botanical road trips as fun as I do, I'm not sure. Towards the end of our recent trip to California, he did say that travelling with me was 'like being in an episode of *Survivor*'. He survived, just.

A commitment to curiosity, honesty and beauty draw us together as collaborators. In Daniel, I've found someone who is on the same (rather unlikely) page as me. Working on this project with him has made me realise how lucky I am. This book would be dreadful without him.

danielshipp.com

DANIEL ON GEORGINA

I couldn't have done the kilometres or the hours that this book required with anyone who wasn't smart and hilarious. George has made the stories in this book happen with her somewhat awkward charm and the endearing (yet fierce) purity of her intentions. Her sense of purpose permeates the air and, like the subjects in this book, I've learnt to let go and trust it.

If you ever visit a nursery with George and can't find her, head to the half-dead plants section. She feels a genuine empathy and love for these unruly 'reduced to clear' specimens because they speak to the values at her core and her irreverent idea of beauty. It's a refreshing approach to life in general, and a lovely 'fuck you' to the popular idea that plants are only valuable as decorative, trend-based or productive objects. This irreverence is where we really connect – our shared explorations of alternate ideas of beauty have impressed a wild, joyful stamp on my soul and my creative vision.

theplanthunter.com.au

PLANT HOPE.